DORLING KINDERSLEY **DK** EYEWITNESS BOOKS

OCEAN

Sea slug

Red seaweed

Lesser
octopus

Cuttlefish

Fishing
trawler

INS 123

Masked crab

Boar fish

European
spiny lobster

EYEWITNESS BOOKS

OCEAN

Written by
DR. MIRANDA MACQUITTY

Photographed by
FRANK GREENAWAY

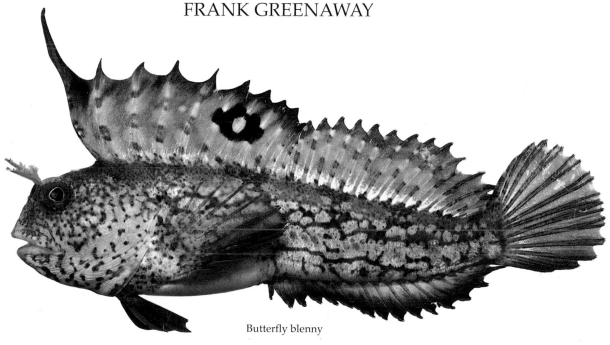
Butterfly blenny

Maerl
seaweed

Common
sea urchin

Dorling Kindersley

Common
sun star

Parchment worm
inside its tube

Red
cushion
star

Dorling Kindersley

**LONDON, NEW YORK, AUCKLAND, DELHI,
JOHANNESBURG, MUNICH, PARIS and SYDNEY**

For a full catalog, visit
DK www.dk.com

Project editor Marion Dent
Art editor Jane Tetzlaff
Managing editor Gillian Denton
Managing art editor Julia Harris
Research Céline Carez
Picture research Kathy Lockley
Production Catherine Semark
Special thanks The University Marine Biological
Station (Scotland), and Sea Life Centres (UK)

This Eyewitness ® Book has been conceived by
Dorling Kindersley Limited and Editions Gallimard

© 1995 Dorling Kindersley Limited
This edition © 2000 Dorling Kindersley Limited
First American edition, 1995

Published in the United States by
Dorling Kindersley Publishing, Inc.
95 Madison Avenue
New York, NY 10016
4 6 8 10 9 7 5 3

Dorling Kindersley books are available at special discounts for bulk
purchases for sales promotions or premiums. Special editions,
including personalized covers, excerpts of existing guides, and
corporate imprints can be created in large quantities for specific
needs. For more information, contact Special Markets Dept., Dorling
Kindersley Publishing, Inc., 95 Madison Ave., New York,
NY 10016; Fax: (800) 600-9098

Library of Congress Cataloging-in-Publication Data
MacQuitty, Miranda.
Ocean / written by Miranda MacQuitty;
photography by Frank Greenaway.
p. cm. — (Eyewitness Books)
Includes Index.
1. Ocean—Juvenile literature. [1. Marine life.] I. Title.
GC21.5.M33 2000   551.46—dc20   95-1477
ISBN 0-7894-6035-1 (pb)
ISBN 0-7894-6472-1 (hc)

Color reproduction by Colourscan, Singapore
Printed in China by Toppan Printing Co. (Shenzhen) Ltd.

Mussel shells

Red
cushion
star

Microscope used
in the late 1800s

Prepared slides

Common sun star

Dead-man's
fingers

Blood
star

Juvenile lumpsucker

Victorian
collection of
shells

Preserving jar
containing a
Norwegian
lobster

Contents

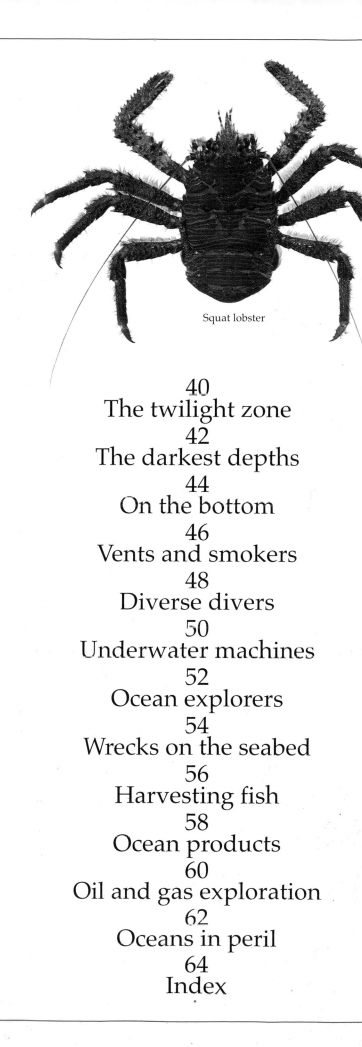

Squat lobster

Oceans of the past

THE EARTH, WITH ITS VAST EXPANSES of ocean, has not always looked the way it does today. Water in the form of vapor was present in the atmosphere of the early earth. As the earth cooled, water vapor condensed, making storm clouds. Rain fell from these clouds and filled the first oceans. Over millions of years the land-masses have drifted across the face of the earth as new oceans opened up and old oceans disappeared. Today's oceans took shape only over the last 200 million years of the earth's 4.5-billion-year existence. As the oceans themselves changed, so too did life within the oceans. Simple organisms first appeared 3.3 billion years ago and were followed by more and more complex life forms. Some forms of life became extinct, but others still survive in the ocean today, more or less unchanged.

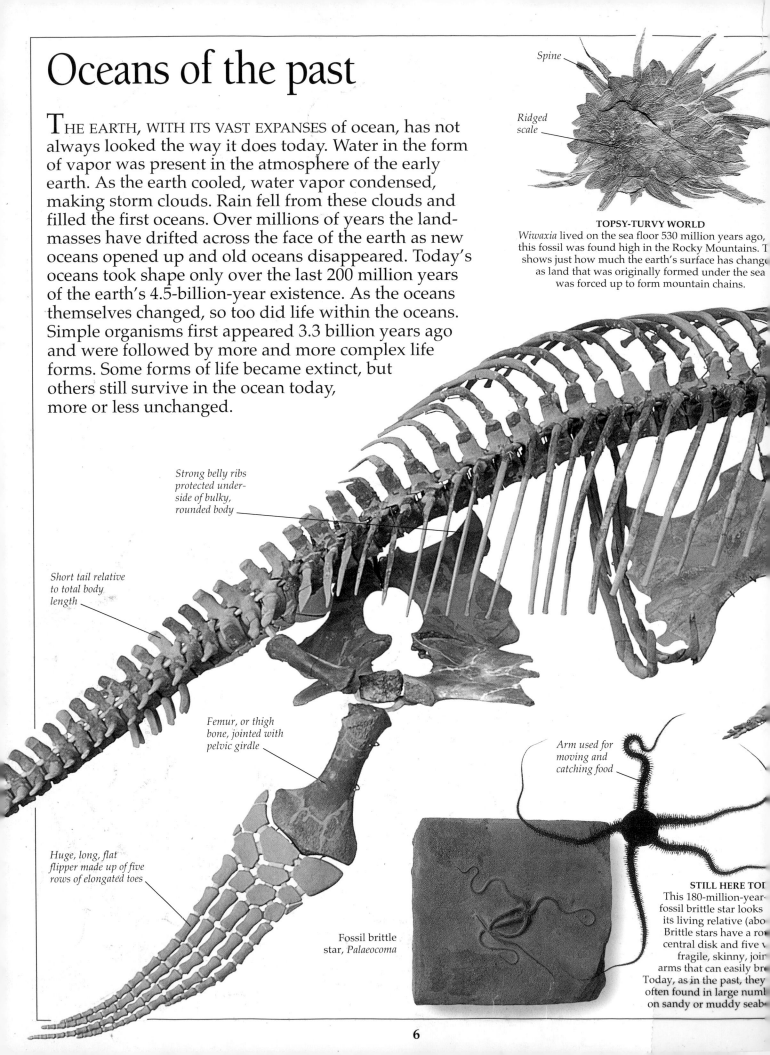

Spine

Ridged scale

TOPSY-TURVY WORLD
Wiwaxia lived on the sea floor 530 million years ago,
this fossil was found high in the Rocky Mountains. T
shows just how much the earth's surface has change
as land that was originally formed under the sea
was forced up to form mountain chains.

Strong belly ribs protected under-side of bulky, rounded body

Short tail relative to total body length

Femur, or thigh bone, jointed with pelvic girdle

Arm used for moving and catching food

Huge, long, flat flipper made up of five rows of elongated toes

Fossil brittle star, *Palaeocoma*

STILL HERE TO
This 180-million-year-
fossil brittle star looks
its living relative (abo
Brittle stars have a ro
central disk and five v
fragile, skinny, join
arms that can easily br
Today, as in the past, they
often found in large numl
on sandy or muddy seab

ANCIENT CORAL
Compared to their soft-bodied relatives, the anemones and jellyfish, corals preserve well as fossils in rocks because of their hard skeletons, such as this 400-million-year-old fossil coral. Each coral animal formed a skeleton joining that of its neighbor to create chains with large spaces between them.

CHANGING OCEANS
One giant ocean, Panthalassa, surrounded the supercontinent Pangaea (1) 290–240 million years ago (mya). At the end of this period, many kinds of marine life became extinct. Pangaea broke up, with part drifting north and part south, with the Tethys Sea between.

CONTINENTAL DRIFT
The northern part split to form the North Atlantic 208–146 mya (2). The South Atlantic and Indian oceans began to form 146–65 mya (3). The continents continued to drift 1.65 mya (4). Today the oceans are still changing shape – the Atlantic ocean gets wider by a few inches each year.

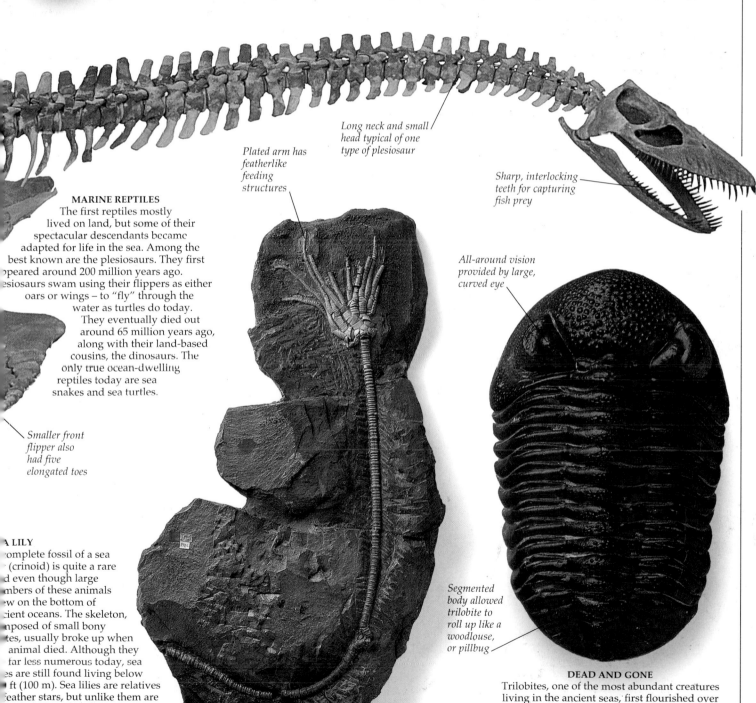

Long neck and small head typical of one type of plesiosaur

Plated arm has featherlike feeding structures

Sharp, interlocking teeth for capturing fish prey

MARINE REPTILES
The first reptiles mostly lived on land, but some of their spectacular descendants became adapted for life in the sea. Among the best known are the plesiosaurs. They first appeared around 200 million years ago. Plesiosaurs swam using their flippers as either oars or wings – to "fly" through the water as turtles do today. They eventually died out around 65 million years ago, along with their land-based cousins, the dinosaurs. The only true ocean-dwelling reptiles today are sea snakes and sea turtles.

Smaller front flipper also had five elongated toes

All-around vision provided by large, curved eye

[SE]A LILY
[A c]omplete fossil of a sea [lily] (crinoid) is quite a rare [find] even though large [num]bers of these animals [gre]w on the bottom of [an]cient oceans. The skeleton, [com]posed of small bony [pla]tes, usually broke up when [the] animal died. Although they [are f]ar less numerous today, sea [lili]es are still found living below [300] ft (100 m). Sea lilies are relatives [of f]eather stars, but unlike them are [usu]ally anchored to the seabed. [The]ir arms surround an upward-[fac]ing mouth and are used to trap [sm]all particles of food drifting by.

Long, flexible stem anchored crinoid in seabed gardens

Segmented body allowed trilobite to roll up like a woodlouse, or pillbug

DEAD AND GONE
Trilobites, one of the most abundant creatures living in the ancient seas, first flourished over 510 million years ago. They had jointed limbs and an external skeleton like insects or crustaceans, such as crabs and lobsters. They died out some 250 million years ago.

Oceans today

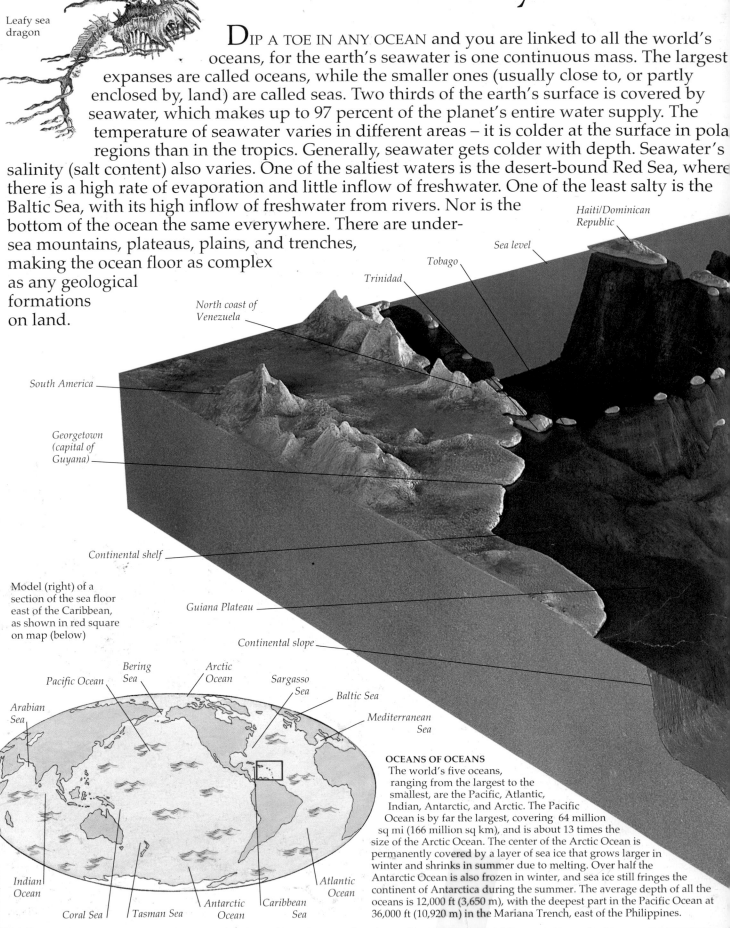

Leafy sea dragon

Dɪᴘ ᴀ ᴛᴏᴇ ɪɴ ᴀɴʏ ᴏᴄᴇᴀɴ and you are linked to all the world's oceans, for the earth's seawater is one continuous mass. The largest expanses are called oceans, while the smaller ones (usually close to, or partly enclosed by, land) are called seas. Two thirds of the earth's surface is covered by seawater, which makes up to 97 percent of the planet's entire water supply. The temperature of seawater varies in different areas – it is colder at the surface in polar regions than in the tropics. Generally, seawater gets colder with depth. Seawater's salinity (salt content) also varies. One of the saltiest waters is the desert-bound Red Sea, where there is a high rate of evaporation and little inflow of freshwater. One of the least salty is the Baltic Sea, with its high inflow of freshwater from rivers. Nor is the bottom of the ocean the same everywhere. There are under-sea mountains, plateaus, plains, and trenches, making the ocean floor as complex as any geological formations on land.

Haiti/Dominican Republic

Sea level

Tobago

Trinidad

North coast of Venezuela

South America

Georgetown (capital of Guyana)

Continental shelf

Model (right) of a section of the sea floor east of the Caribbean, as shown in red square on map (below)

Guiana Plateau

Continental slope

Bering Sea

Arctic Ocean

Sargasso Sea

Pacific Ocean

Baltic Sea

Arabian Sea

Mediterranean Sea

Indian Ocean

Atlantic Ocean

Coral Sea

Tasman Sea

Antarctic Ocean

Caribbean Sea

OCEANS OF OCEANS

The world's five oceans, ranging from the largest to the smallest, are the Pacific, Atlantic, Indian, Antarctic, and Arctic. The Pacific Ocean is by far the largest, covering 64 million sq mi (166 million sq km), and is about 13 times the size of the Arctic Ocean. The center of the Arctic Ocean is permanently covered by a layer of sea ice that grows larger in winter and shrinks in summer due to melting. Over half the Antarctic Ocean is also frozen in winter, and sea ice still fringes the continent of Antarctica during the summer. The average depth of all the oceans is 12,000 ft (3,650 m), with the deepest part in the Pacific Ocean at 36,000 ft (10,920 m) in the Mariana Trench, east of the Philippines.

SEA OR LAKE?
The water in the Dead Sea is saltier than any ocean because the water that drains into it evaporates in the hot sun, leaving behind the salts. A body is more buoyant in such salty water, making it easier to float. The Dead Sea is a lake, not a sea, because it is completely surrounded by land. True seas are always connected to the ocean by a channel.

Floating on the
Dead Sea

GOD OF THE WATERS
Neptune, the Roman god of the sea, is usually shown riding a dolphin and carrying a trident (pronged spear). It was thought he controlled freshwater supplies, so offerings were made to him at the driest time of the year.

DISAPPEARING ACT
The gigantic plates on the earth's crust move like a conveyor belt. As new areas of ocean floor form at spreading centers, old areas disappear into the molten heart of the planet. This diagram shows one oceanic plate being forced under another (subduction) in the Mariana Trench, creating an island arc.

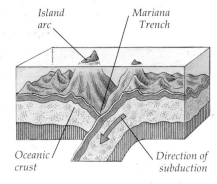

Island arc

Mariana Trench

Oceanic crust

Direction of subduction

Formation of Mariana Trench

Hatteras Abyssal Plain

Puerto Rico Trench

Nares Abyssal Plain

Mid-Atlantic Ridge

Kane fracture zone

Vema fracture zone

Demerara Abyssal Plain

THE OCEAN FLOOR
This model shows the features on the bottom of the Atlantic Ocean off the northeast coast of South America from Guyana to Venezuela. Off this coast is the continental shelf, a region of relatively shallow water about 660 ft (200 m) deep. Here the continental shelf is about 125 mi (200 km) wide, whereas that off the coast of northern Asia is as much as 1,000 mi (1,600 km) wide. At the outer edge of the continental shelf, the ocean floor drops away steeply to form the continental slope. Sediments eroded from the land and carried by rivers, such as the Orinoco, accumulate at the bottom of this continental slope. The ocean floor then opens out in virtually flat areas, known as abyssal plains, which are covered with a deep layer of soft sediments. The Puerto Rico Trench is formed where one of the earth's plates (the North American plate) is sliding past another (the Caribbean plate). An arc of volcanic islands have also been created where the North American plate is forced under the Caribbean plate. The fracture zones are offsets of the Mid-Atlantic Ridge.

Life in the oceans

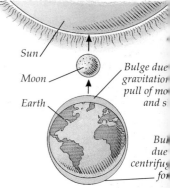

Fᴿᴏᴍ ᴛʜᴇ ꜱᴇᴀꜱʜᴏʀᴇ to the deepest depths, oceans are home to some of the most diverse life on earth. Animals live either on the seabed or in midwater, where they swim or float. Plants are only found in the sunlit zone, where there is enough light for growth. Animals are found at all depths of the oceans, though are most abundant in the sunlit zone, where food is plentiful. Not all free-swimming animals stay in one zone – the sperm whale dives to over 1,640 ft (500 m) to feed on squid, returning to the surface to breathe air. Some animals from cold, deep waters, such as the Greenland shark in the Atlantic, are also found in the cold surface waters of polar regions. Over 90 percent of all species dwell on the bottom. A single rock can be home to over ten major groups, such as corals, mollusks, and sponges. Most ocean animals and plants have their origins in the sea, but some, such as whales and sea grasses, are descended from ancestors that once lived on land.

Blood star

Common sun star

SHORE LIFE
Often found on the shore at low tide, starfish also live in deeper water. Sea life on the shore must either be tough enough to withstand drying out, or find shelter in rock pools. The toughest animals and plants live high on the shore. The least able to cope in air are found at the bottom.

Sun
Moon
Earth
Bulge due gravitation pull of mo and s
Bu due centrifug fo

TIME AND TII
Anyone spending time the beach or in an estuary w notice the tides. Tides are cause by the gravitational pull of t moon on the earth's mass seawater. An equal and opposi bulge of water occurs on the si of the earth away from the moo due to centrifugal force. As t earth spins on its axis, the bulg (high tides) usually occur twice day in any one place. The highe and lowest tides occur whe the moon and sun are in lir causing the greatest gravitation pull. These are the spring tid at new and full moo

SQUISHY SQUI
Squid are among the mo common animals living in t ocean. Like fish, they oft swim around in schools f protection in number Their torpedo-shape bodies are streamline so they can swim fa

Inside squid's soft body is a horny, penlike shell

Tentacles reach out to grasp food

Deep-sea cat shark grows to only 20 in (50 cm) long

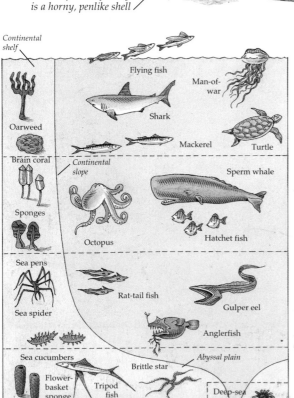

Continental shelf
Flying fish
Man-of-war
Shark
Oarweed
Mackerel
Turtle
Brain coral
Continental slope
Sperm whale
Sponges
Octopus
Hatchet fish
Sea pens
Rat-tail fish
Sea spider
Gulper eel
Anglerfish
Sea cucumbers
Abyssal plain
Brittle star
Flower-basket sponge
Tripod fish
Deep-sea anemone

Note: Neither the marine life or zones are drawn to scale

Sunlit zone
0–660 ft
(0–200 m)

Twilight zone
660–3,300 ft
(200–1,000 m)

Dark zone
3,300–13,200 ft
(1,000–4,000 m)

Abyss
13,200–19,800 ft
(4,000–6,000 m)

Trench
Over 19,800 ft
(6,000 m)

THE OCEAN'S ZONES
The ocean is divided up into broad zones, according to how far down sunlight penetrates and the water temperature. In the sunl zone, there is plenty of light, much water movement, and season changes in temperature. Beneath this is the twilight zone, the maximum depth to which light penetrates. Temperatures here decrease rapidly with depth to about 41°F (5°C). Deeper yet is the dark zone, where there is no light and temperatures drop to abou 34–36°F (1–2°C). Still in darkness and even deeper is the abyss, while the deepest part of the ocean occurs in the trenches. There are also zones on the seabed. The shallowest zone ranges from th low-tide mark to the edge of the continental shelf. Below this are the zones of the continental slope and finally the abyssal plains.

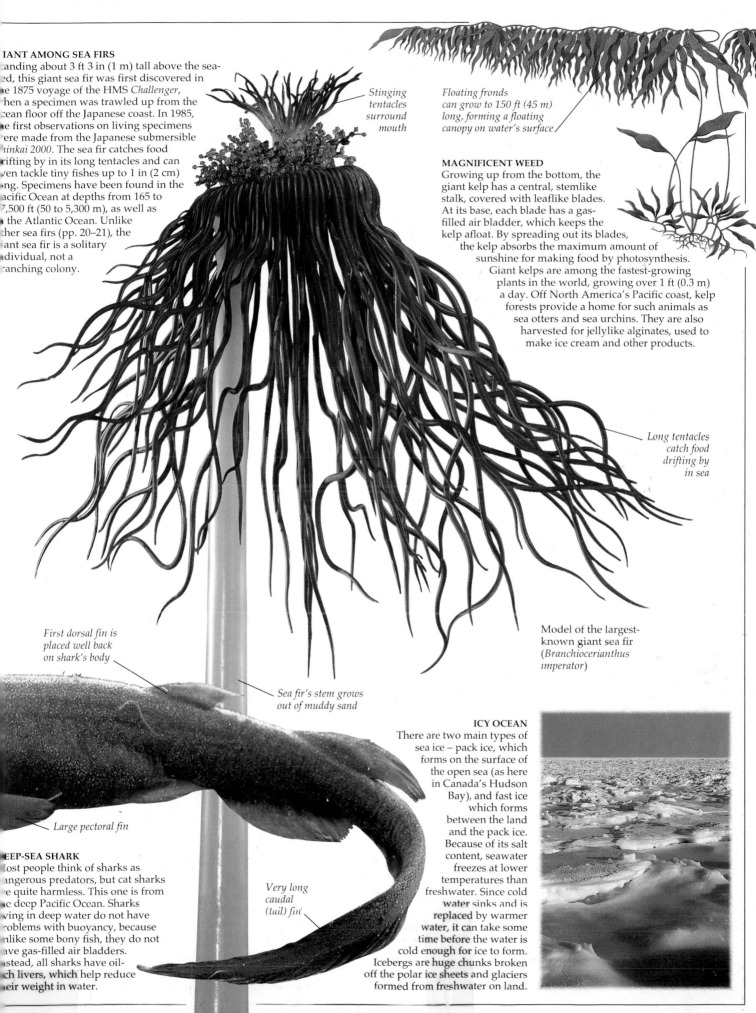

GIANT AMONG SEA FIRS

Standing about 3 ft 3 in (1 m) tall above the seabed, this giant sea fir was first discovered in
the 1875 voyage of the HMS *Challenger*,
when a specimen was trawled up from the
ocean floor off the Japanese coast. In 1985,
the first observations on living specimens
were made from the Japanese submersible
Shinkai 2000. The sea fir catches food
drifting by in its long tentacles and can
even tackle tiny fishes up to 1 in (2 cm)
long. Specimens have been found in the
Pacific Ocean at depths from 165 to
17,500 ft (50 to 5,300 m), as well as
in the Atlantic Ocean. Unlike
other sea firs (pp. 20–21), the
giant sea fir is a solitary
individual, not a
branching colony.

*Stinging
tentacles
surround
mouth*

*Floating fronds
can grow to 150 ft (45 m)
long, forming a floating
canopy on water's surface*

MAGNIFICENT WEED

Growing up from the bottom, the
giant kelp has a central, stemlike
stalk, covered with leaflike blades.
At its base, each blade has a gas-
filled air bladder, which keeps the
kelp afloat. By spreading out its blades,
the kelp absorbs the maximum amount of
sunshine for making food by photosynthesis.
Giant kelps are among the fastest-growing
plants in the world, growing over 1 ft (0.3 m)
a day. Off North America's Pacific coast, kelp
forests provide a home for such animals as
sea otters and sea urchins. They are also
harvested for jellylike alginates, used to
make ice cream and other products.

*Long tentacles
catch food
drifting by
in sea*

*First dorsal fin is
placed well back
on shark's body*

*Sea fir's stem grows
out of muddy sand*

Model of the largest-
known giant sea fir
(*Branchiocerianthus
imperator*)

Large pectoral fin

DEEP-SEA SHARK

Most people think of sharks as
dangerous predators, but cat sharks
are quite harmless. This one is from
the deep Pacific Ocean. Sharks
living in deep water do not have
problems with buoyancy, because
unlike some bony fish, they do not
have gas-filled air bladders.
Instead, all sharks have oil-
rich livers, which help reduce
their weight in water.

*Very long
caudal
(tail) fin*

ICY OCEAN

There are two main types of
sea ice – pack ice, which
forms on the surface of
the open sea (as here
in Canada's Hudson
Bay), and fast ice
which forms
between the land
and the pack ice.
Because of its salt
content, seawater
freezes at lower
temperatures than
freshwater. Since cold
water sinks and is
replaced by warmer
water, it can take some
time before the water is
cold enough for ice to form.
Icebergs are huge chunks broken
off the polar ice sheets and glaciers
formed from freshwater on land.

Waves and weather

SEAWATER IS CONSTANTLY moving, and waves can be 50-ft (15-m) troughs. Major surface currents are driven by the earth's winds, including trade winds, which blow toward the equator. Both surface and deep-water currents affect the world's climate by taking cold water from the polar regions toward the tropics, and vice versa. Shifts in this flow can also affect ocean life. In an El Niño (climate change), trade winds diminish and warm water flows down western South America. This stops nutrient-rich, cold water from rising up and cause plankton and fisheries to fail. Heat from oceans creates air movement, like swirling hurricanes. Daytime onshore breezes form when the ocean heats up more slowly than the land in the day. Cool air above the water blows in, replacing warm air above the land. At night, offshore breezes occur when the reverse happens.

DOWN THE SPOU
Water spouts (spinning spra
sucked up from the surface) beg
when whirling air drops dov
from a storm cloud to the ocea

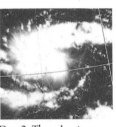

Day 2: Thunderstorms
as swirling cloud mass

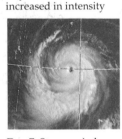

Day 4: Winds have
increased in intensity

Day 7: Strong winds

A HURRICANE IS BORN
These satellite photographs show a hurricane developing. On day 2 a swirling cloud mass is formed. By day 4 fierce winds develop at the center. By day 7 winds are the strongest.

RIVERS OF THE SEA
Currents are huge masses of water moving through the oceans. The course currents follow is not precisely the same as the trade winds and westerlies, because currents are deflected off land and the Coriolis force produced by the earth's rotation. The latter causes currents to shift to the right in the Northern Hemisphere and to the left in the Southern. There are also currents that flow due to differences in density of seawater.

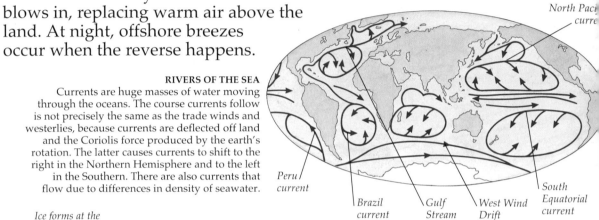

North Pac
curre

Peru
current

Brazil
current

Gulf
Stream

West Wind
Drift

South
Equatorial
current

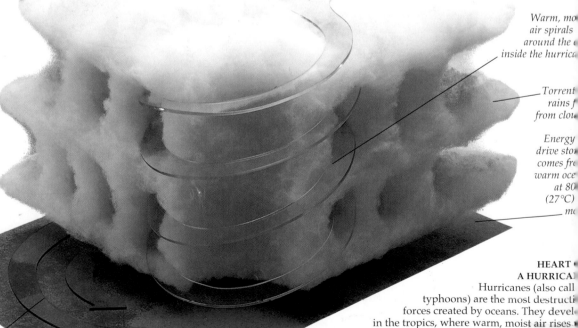

Ice forms at the
very top of the
clouds

Hurricanes are enormo
– some may be 500 mi
(800 k
acr

Warm, mo
air spirals
around the (
inside the hurric

Torrent
rains f
from clou

Energy
drive sto
comes fr
warm oce
at 80
(27°C)
m

HEART
A HURRICA
Hurricanes (also call typhoons) are the most destructi forces created by oceans. They devel in the tropics, where warm, moist air rises from the ocean's surface and creates storm clou As more air spirals upward, energy is released, fueli stronger winds that whirl around the "eye" (a calm area extreme low pressure). Hurricanes move onto land, causin terrible devastation. Away from the ocean, hurricanes die o

Strongest winds of up to
220 mph (360 kph) occur
just outside the eye

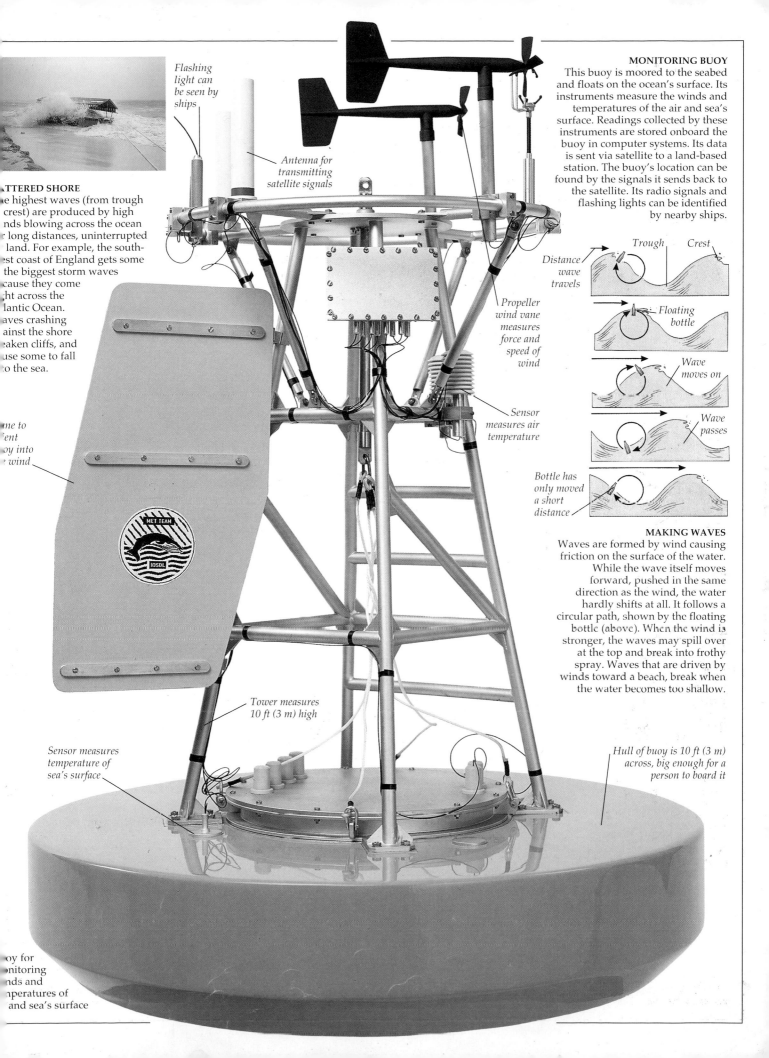

Flashing light can be seen by ships

Antenna for transmitting satellite signals

MONITORING BUOY

This buoy is moored to the seabed and floats on the ocean's surface. Its instruments measure the winds and temperatures of the air and sea's surface. Readings collected by these instruments are stored onboard the buoy in computer systems. Its data is sent via satellite to a land-based station. The buoy's location can be found by the signals it sends back to the satellite. Its radio signals and flashing lights can be identified by nearby ships.

Propeller wind vane measures force and speed of wind

Sensor measures air temperature

Distance wave travels

Trough   Crest

Floating bottle

Wave moves on

Wave passes

Bottle has only moved a short distance

MAKING WAVES

Waves are formed by wind causing friction on the surface of the water. While the wave itself moves forward, pushed in the same direction as the wind, the water hardly shifts at all. It follows a circular path, shown by the floating bottle (above). When the wind is stronger, the waves may spill over at the top and break into frothy spray. Waves that are driven by winds toward a beach, break when the water becomes too shallow.

...TTERED SHORE

...e highest waves (from trough ... crest) are produced by high ...nds blowing across the ocean ... long distances, uninterrupted ... land. For example, the south-...st coast of England gets some ... the biggest storm waves ...cause they come ...ht across the ...lantic Ocean. ...aves crashing ...ainst the shore ...eaken cliffs, and ...use some to fall ... the sea.

...ne to
...ent
...oy into
...e wind

MET TEAM
IOSDL

Tower measures 10 ft (3 m) high

Sensor measures temperature of sea's surface

Hull of buoy is 10 ft (3 m) across, big enough for a person to board it

...oy for
...nitoring
...ds and
...peratures of
...and sea's surface

Sandy and muddy

IN SHALLOW COASTAL WATERS, from the lowest part of the shore to the edge of the continental shelf, sand and mud are washed from the land, creating vast stretches of sea floor that look like underwater deserts. Without rocks, there are no abundant growths of seaweeds to hide among, so animals that move above the sandy floor are exposed to predators. Many creatures protect themselves by burrowing in the soft seabed. Some worms hide inside their own tubes and feed by spreading out a fan of tentacles or by drawing water containing food particles into their tubes. Other worms, such as the sea mouse, move around in search of food. Flatfish (fish with eyes on one side of the head in the adult, like a flounder) are common on the sandy seabed, looking for any readily available food, such as peacock worms. All the animals shown here live in the coastal waters of the Atlantic Ocean.

Tough papery tube protects soft worm inside

Worm can grow up to 16 in (40 cm) long

Bulky body covered by dense mat of fine hairs

Coarse, shiny bristles help it move along seabed

BEAUTIFUL BRISTLE WO[RM]
The sea mouse, or bristle wor[m], plows its way through muddy sa[nd] on the seabed and is often washed up o[n] the beach after storms. The shiny, rainbow-colore[d] spines help propel it along and may make this chun[ky] worm less appetizing to fish. The sea mouse usually keeps its rear end out of the sand to bring in a stre[am] of fresh seawater to help it breathe. Sea mice grow to 4 in (10 cm) long and eat any dead animals they may find in the sand.

Light color helps it merge into sand

Thick trunk looks like peanut when body retracts

Surface of plump, unsegmented body feels rough

PEANUT WORM
Many different kinds of worms live in the sea. This is one of the sipunculid worms, sometimes called peanut worms. Its stretchy front part can retract into its thicker trunk. Peanut worms usually burrow in sand and mud, but some of the 320 kinds of peanut worm live in empty sea shells and in coral crevices.

Front part can also retract

Poisonous spines on first dorsal fin

Poisonous spine on front of gill cover

High-set eye allows all-around vision

Mouth surrounded by tentacles

WARY WEEVER
When a weever fish is buried in sand, its eyes on top of its head help it see what is going on. The weever's strategically placed poisonous spines provide it with extra defense. Its spines can inflict nasty wounds on humans if it is accidentally stepped on in shallow water or caught in fishermen's nets.

FLATFISH
Flounders cruise along the se[a] looking for food. They can ni[p] the tops off peacock worms if [they] are quick enough to catch th[em]

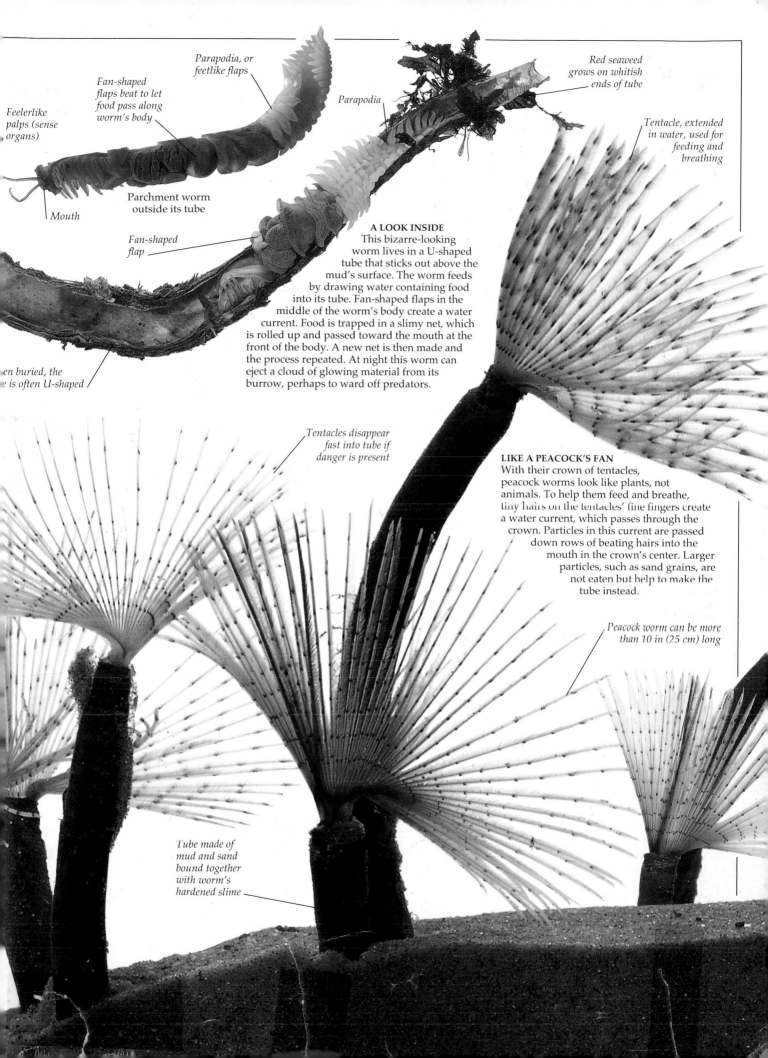

Feelerlike
palps (sense
organs)

Fan-shaped
flaps beat to let
food pass along
worm's body

Parapodia, or
feetlike flaps

Parapodia

Red seaweed
grows on whitish
ends of tube

Tentacle, extended
in water, used for
feeding and
breathing

Mouth

Parchment worm
outside its tube

Fan-shaped
flap

...en buried, the
...e is often U-shaped

A LOOK INSIDE
This bizarre-looking
worm lives in a U-shaped
tube that sticks out above the
mud's surface. The worm feeds
by drawing water containing food
into its tube. Fan-shaped flaps in the
middle of the worm's body create a water
current. Food is trapped in a slimy net, which
is rolled up and passed toward the mouth at the
front of the body. A new net is then made and
the process repeated. At night this worm can
eject a cloud of glowing material from its
burrow, perhaps to ward off predators.

Tentacles disappear
fast into tube if
danger is present

LIKE A PEACOCK'S FAN
With their crown of tentacles,
peacock worms look like plants, not
animals. To help them feed and breathe,
tiny hairs on the tentacles' fine fingers create
a water current, which passes through the
crown. Particles in this current are passed
down rows of beating hairs into the
mouth in the crown's center. Larger
particles, such as sand grains, are
not eaten but help to make the
tube instead.

Peacock worm can be more
than 10 in (25 cm) long

Tube made of
mud and sand
bound together
with worm's
hardened slime

Soft seabed

SWIMMING OVER a soft seabed, using a mask and snorkel, it is possible to see only a few animals because most of them live buried in the sand. Look closely and you may see signs of this buried life, such as clams' siphons or a crab's feathery antennae, poking through the sand to help get clean supplies of oxygen-containing water. Some fish, like the eagle ray, visit the soft seabed to feed on burrowing clams. Other animals are found only where sea grasses grow on sandy bottoms. Sea grasses are not seaweeds but flowering plants. They are food for many animals, including the dugong – the only plant-eating mammal that truly lives in the sea.

Tough skin protects dugong

DOCILE DUGONG
Dugongs live in shallow tropical waters, where they feed on sea grasses growing in the soft seabed. They often dig down into the sand to eat the food-rich roots of sea grasses. These gentle, shy animals are still hunted in some places.

SHELL BOAT
In Botticelli's *The Birth of Venus*, the Roma goddess rises from the water in a scallop shell. In real life, scallop shells found in th soft seabed are too heavy to float.

This sea pen can grow to 8 in (20 cm) in height

ELEGANT PEN
Looking like an old-fashioned quill pen, this relative of the sea anemone (pp. 28–29) lives in the soft seabed. Rows of tiny polyps, or buds, on each side of its body are used to capture small animals drifting by for food. Sea pens glow in the dark if disturbed. Some sea pens grow on the bottom of the deep ocean.

Anemone-like polyp unfurls when feeding

Long dorsal fin runs along almost whole length of body

RED BAND FISH
This fish usually lives i burrows in the soft seab down to depths of abou 660 ft (200 m). It is als found swimming amor sea grasses. Sometimes band fish are found wash up on the beach after storms. Out of ifs burro the fish swims by passi waves down its body. feeds on small animal drifting by.

Long anal fin

Red band fish may grow to 28 in (70 cm) in length

Stem of sea pen anchors in sandy seabed

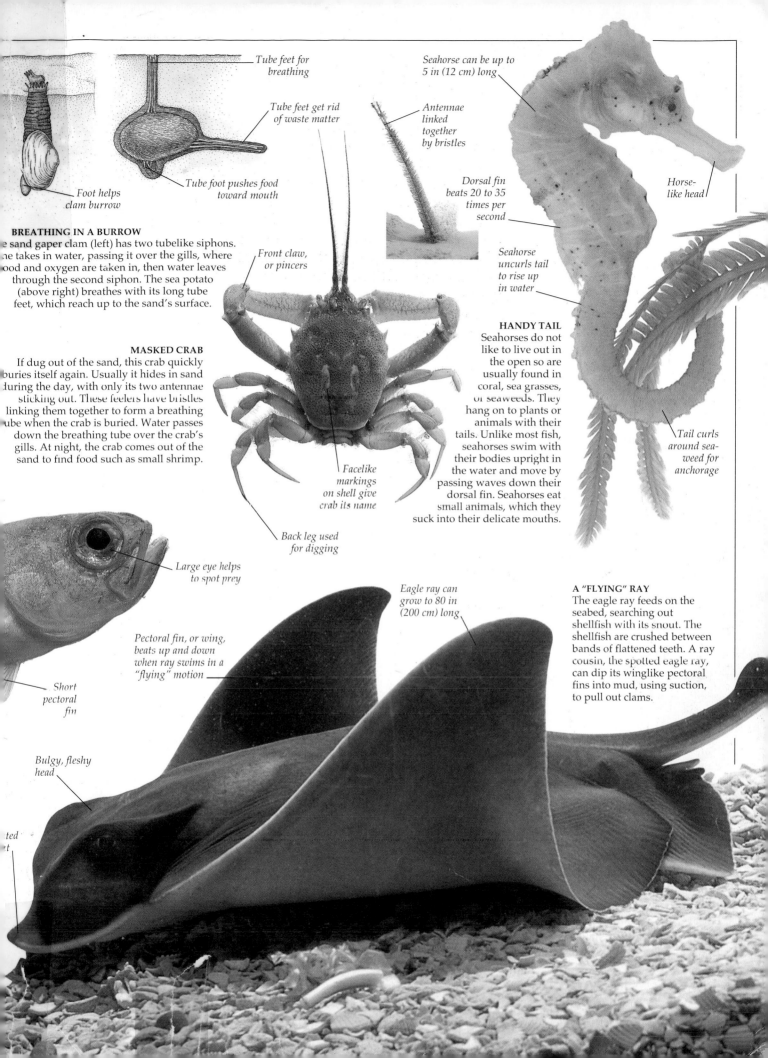

Tube feet for breathing

Tube feet get rid of waste matter

Tube foot pushes food toward mouth

Foot helps clam burrow

BREATHING IN A BURROW
[Th]e sand gaper clam (left) has two tubelike siphons. [I]t takes in water, passing it over the gills, where [fo]od and oxygen are taken in, then water leaves through the second siphon. The sea potato (above right) breathes with its long tube feet, which reach up to the sand's surface.

Antennae linked together by bristles

Seahorse can be up to 5 in (12 cm) long

Horse-like head

Dorsal fin beats 20 to 35 times per second

Seahorse uncurls tail to rise up in water

Front claw, or pincers

MASKED CRAB
If dug out of the sand, this crab quickly [b]uries itself again. Usually it hides in sand [d]uring the day, with only its two antennae [s]ticking out. These feelers have bristles linking them together to form a breathing [t]ube when the crab is buried. Water passes down the breathing tube over the crab's gills. At night, the crab comes out of the sand to find food such as small shrimp.

HANDY TAIL
Seahorses do not like to live out in the open so are usually found in coral, sea grasses, or seaweeds. They hang on to plants or animals with their tails. Unlike most fish, seahorses swim with their bodies upright in the water and move by passing waves down their dorsal fin. Seahorses eat small animals, which they suck into their delicate mouths.

Tail curls around sea-weed for anchorage

Facelike markings on shell give crab its name

Back leg used for digging

Large eye helps to spot prey

Short pectoral fin

Pectoral fin, or wing, beats up and down when ray swims in a "flying" motion

Eagle ray can grow to 80 in (200 cm) long

A "FLYING" RAY
The eagle ray feeds on the seabed, searching out shellfish with its snout. The shellfish are crushed between bands of flattened teeth. A ray cousin, the spotted eagle ray, can dip its winglike pectoral fins into mud, using suction, to pull out clams.

Bulgy, fleshy head

Rocks underwater

ROCKY SEABEDS are found in coastal waters where currents sweep away any sand and mud. With the strong water movement, animals have to cling on to the rocks, find crevices to hide in, or take shelter among seaweeds. A few remarkable animals, such as the clamlike piddocks and some sea urchins, can bore into solid rock to make their homes. Sea urchins bore cavities in hard rock, while piddocks drill into softer rocks such as sandstone or chalk. Some creatures hide under smaller stones, but only if they are lodged in the soft seabed. When masses of loose pebbles roll around, animals and seaweeds can be crushed. However, some crustaceans, such as lobsters, can regain a lost limb crushed by a stone, and starfish can even regrow a missing arm. Some animals can survive at the seashore's edge, especially in rock pools, but many need to stay submerged.

Sea urchin boring into rocks

Piddock

ROCK BORERS
Some sea urchins use their spines and teeth beneath their shells to bore spaces in rock, while piddocks drill with the tips of their shells. Using its muscular foot, the piddock twists and turns to drill and hold on to its burrow. Both are found in shallow water and on the lower shore.

Dorsal fin has eyespot to frig[hten] predators

BEAUTIFUL BUTTERFLY
Blennies, small fish living in shallow water, often rest on the bottom and hide in crannies. They lay their eggs in sheltered places, such as abandoned bottles, and guard them from predators. Blennies feed on small creatures, such as mites, and live on rocky or stony ground to depths of 66 ft (20 m).

Spiny shell helps deter predators

SPINY LOBSTER
European spiny lobsters, or crawfish, are reddish brown in life. With their small pincers, spiny lobsters are restricted to eating soft prey, such as worms or dead animals. They live among rocks, hiding in crevices during the day, but venturing out over the seabed at night to find food. Some kinds of spiny lobsters move in long lines, keeping in touch with the lobster in front with their antennae.

Delicate claw on tip of walking leg

European spiny lobster, also known as a crawfish

Leg used for walking

Tail can be flapped so lobster can swim backward

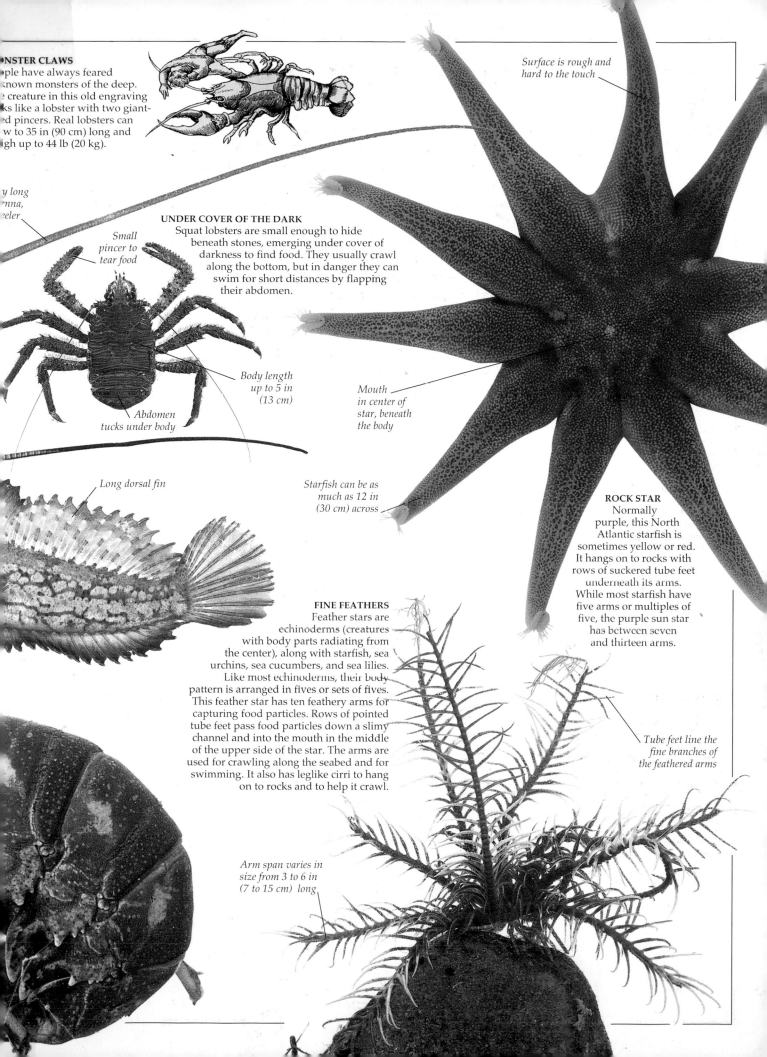

MONSTER CLAWS

...ple have always feared
...known monsters of the deep.
...e creature in this old engraving
...ks like a lobster with two giant-
...d pincers. Real lobsters can
...w to 35 in (90 cm) long and
...gh up to 44 lb (20 kg).

*...y long
...nna,
...eler*

*Surface is rough and
hard to the touch*

*Small
pincer to
tear food*

UNDER COVER OF THE DARK

Squat lobsters are small enough to hide
beneath stones, emerging under cover of
darkness to find food. They usually crawl
along the bottom, but in danger they can
swim for short distances by flapping
their abdomen.

*Body length
up to 5 in
(13 cm)*

*Mouth
in center of
star, beneath
the body*

*Abdomen
tucks under body*

Long dorsal fin

*Starfish can be as
much as 12 in
(30 cm) across*

ROCK STAR

Normally
purple, this North
Atlantic starfish is
sometimes yellow or red.
It hangs on to rocks with
rows of suckered tube feet
underneath its arms.
While most starfish have
five arms or multiples of
five, the purple sun star
has between seven
and thirteen arms.

FINE FEATHERS

Feather stars are
echinoderms (creatures
with body parts radiating from
the center), along with starfish, sea
urchins, sea cucumbers, and sea lilies.
Like most echinoderms, their body
pattern is arranged in fives or sets of fives.
This feather star has ten feathery arms for
capturing food particles. Rows of pointed
tube feet pass food particles down a slimy
channel and into the mouth in the middle
of the upper side of the star. The arms are
used for crawling along the seabed and for
swimming. It also has leglike cirri to hang
on to rocks and to help it crawl.

*Tube feet line the
fine branches of
the feathered arms*

*Arm span varies in
size from 3 to 6 in
(7 to 15 cm) long*

On the rocks

IN THE SHALLOW, COOL WATERS above rocky seabeds, forests of large brown seaweeds called kelp provide a home, hunting ground, and resting place for many creatures. Along North America's Pacific coast, sea otters wrap themselves in kelp and snooze on the surface. At the kelp's base, its holdfast, or rootlike anchor, is home for many animals, such as crabs, and other seaweeds. Unlike the roots of land plants, kelp's holdfast is only an anchor – it does not absorb nutrients o water. Other animals live on the kelp's surface or grow directly onto th rocks, capturing food brought to them in the currents. Sea firs look like plants, but are animals belonging to the same group as sea anemones, jellyfish, and corals, and all have stinging tentacles. Mussels anchored to rocks are shelter for animals that live among, or within, their shells.

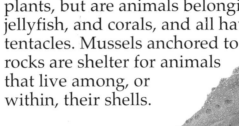

A type of brown seaweed (kelp) found in the Pacific Ocean

DELIGHTFUL MARINE MAMMAL
Sea otters swim and rest among the giant kelp fronds along North America's Pacific coast. They dive down to the seabed to pick up shellfish, smashing them open by banging them against a rock balanced on their chest.

ANCHORED ALGAE
Growing in shallow water, kelp is often battered by waves. Holdfasts of the large, tough, brown algae keep it firmly anchored by tightly gripping the rocks.

Holdfast of oarweed kelp

Holdfast must be strong, as some kinds of kelp can grow over 33 ft (10 m) long

Scaleless body is covered with small warty bumps

Juvenile lumpsucker

PRETTY BA
Young lumpsuck are more beaut than their dun parents, which cling to rocks with sucker fins on their bellies. A lumpsuckers move i shallow water to bre and the father gua the eg

Each stu blunt fir measure least 1.2 (3 cm) ac

Fleshy fingers supported by tiny, hard splinters

W anemone polyp capt food from moving cur

Gills

DEAD-MAN'S FINGERS
When this soft coral is washed up on the shore, its rubbery, fleshy form lives up to its name! Growing on rocks, the colonies consist of many polyps (feeding heads) within a fleshy, orange or white base.

SEA MAT
The lacy-looking growth on the surface of this piece of kelp (left) is a bryozoan, or moss animal. These animals live in colonies where many individuals grow next to each other. Each little compartment houses one of these animals, which come out to feed, capturing food in their tiny tentacles. The colony grows, as individuals bud off new individuals. Other kinds of moss animal grow upward and look a little like seaweeds or corals. Between the sea mats, a blue-rayed limpet grazes on the kelp's surface.

SEA S
Many sea s are meat eaters. slug lives on the coral known as dead-m fingers. Some sea slugs are to eat the stinging tentacle anemones and keep the sti for their own protection. slug eggs hatch into swimm young, which then settle turn into ad

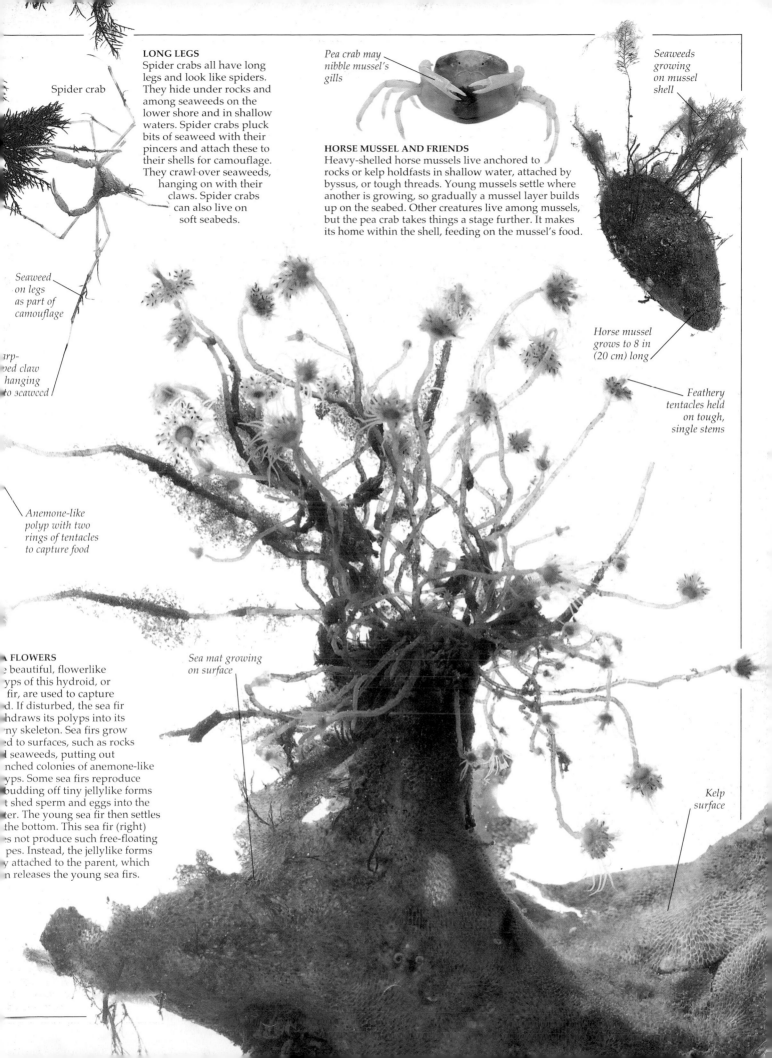

Spider crab

LONG LEGS
Spider crabs all have long legs and look like spiders. They hide under rocks and among seaweeds on the lower shore and in shallow waters. Spider crabs pluck bits of seaweed with their pincers and attach these to their shells for camouflage. They crawl over seaweeds, hanging on with their claws. Spider crabs can also live on soft seabeds.

Pea crab may nibble mussel's gills

HORSE MUSSEL AND FRIENDS
Heavy-shelled horse mussels live anchored to rocks or kelp holdfasts in shallow water, attached by byssus, or tough threads. Young mussels settle where another is growing, so gradually a mussel layer builds up on the seabed. Other creatures live among mussels, but the pea crab takes things a stage further. It makes its home within the shell, feeding on the mussel's food.

Seaweeds growing on mussel shell

Seaweed on legs as part of camouflage

...arp-...ed claw ...hanging ...to seaweed

Horse mussel grows to 8 in (20 cm) long

Feathery tentacles held on tough, single stems

Anemone-like polyp with two rings of tentacles to capture food

...A FLOWERS
...e beautiful, flowerlike ...yps of this hydroid, or ... fir, are used to capture ...d. If disturbed, the sea fir ...hdraws its polyps into its ...ny skeleton. Sea firs grow ...d to surfaces, such as rocks ...d seaweeds, putting out ...nched colonies of anemone-like ...yps. Some sea firs reproduce ...budding off tiny jellylike forms ...t shed sperm and eggs into the ...ter. The young sea fir then settles ...the bottom. This sea fir (right) ...s not produce such free-floating ...pes. Instead, the jellylike forms ...y attached to the parent, which ...n releases the young sea firs.

Sea mat growing on surface

Kelp surface

The coral kingdom

IN THE WARM, CRYSTAL-CLEAR WATERS of the tropics, coral reefs flourish, covering vast areas. Made of the skeletons of stony corals, coral reefs are cemented together by chalky algae. Most stony corals are colonies of many tiny, anemone-like individuals, called polyps. Each polyp makes its own hard limestone cup (skeleton), which protects its soft body. To make their skeletons, the coral polyps need the help of microscopic, single-celled algae that live inside them. The algae need sunlight to grow, which is why coral reefs are found only in sunny, surface waters. In return for giving the algae a home, corals get some food from them but also capture plankton with their tentacles. Only the upper layer of a reef is made of living corals, which build upon skeletons of dead polyps. Coral reefs are also home to soft corals and sea fans, which do not have stony skeletons. Related to sea anemones and jellyfish, corals grow in an exquisite variety of shapes (mushroom, daisy, staghorn) and some have colorful skeletons.

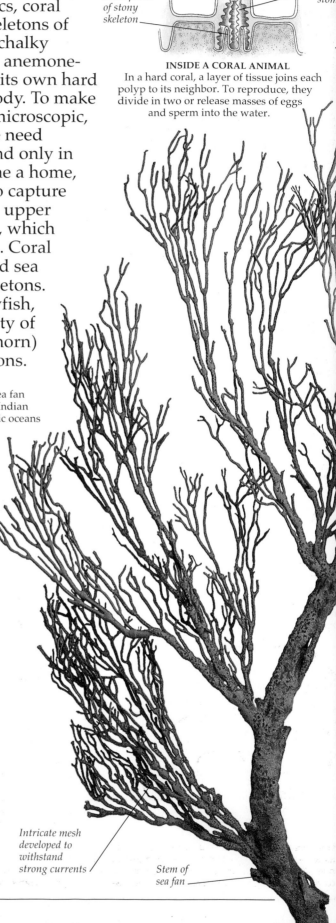

Tentacle's stings catch food

Mouth expels w

Hard plates of stony skeleton

Bag stom

INSIDE A CORAL ANIMAL
In a hard coral, a layer of tissue joins each polyp to its neighbor. To reproduce, they divide in two or release masses of eggs and sperm into the water.

Black coral's horny skeleton looks like a bunch of twigs

Orange sea fan from the Indian and Pacific oceans

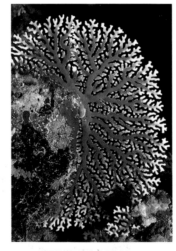

STINGING CORAL
Colorful hydrocorals are related to sea firs and, unlike horny and stony corals, produce jellyfish-like forms that carry their sex organs. Known as fire corals, they have potent stings on their polyps.

BLACK CORAL
In living black corals, the skeleton provides support for the living tissues, and the branches bear rows of anemone-like polyps. Black corals are mainly found in tropical waters, growing in the deep part of coral reefs. Although they take a long time to grow, the black skeleton is sometimes used to make jewelry.

Intricate mesh developed to withstand strong currents

Stem of sea fan

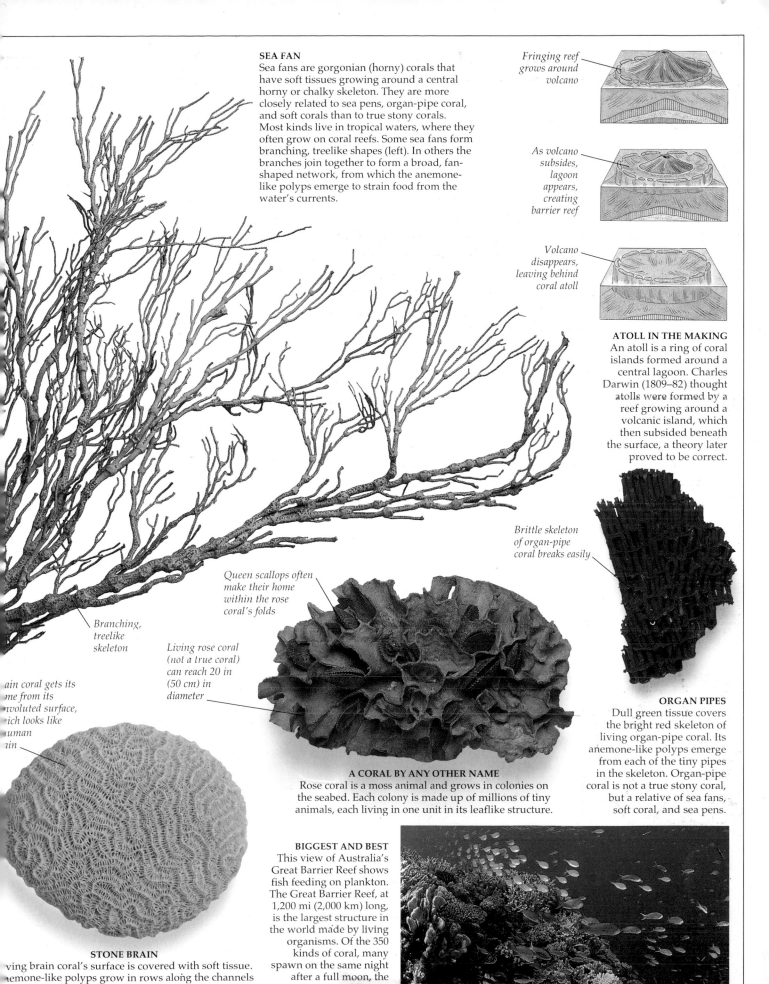

SEA FAN
Sea fans are gorgonian (horny) corals that have soft tissues growing around a central horny or chalky skeleton. They are more closely related to sea pens, organ-pipe coral, and soft corals than to true stony corals. Most kinds live in tropical waters, where they often grow on coral reefs. Some sea fans form branching, treelike shapes (left). In others the branches join together to form a broad, fan-shaped network, from which the anemone-like polyps emerge to strain food from the water's currents.

Fringing reef grows around volcano

As volcano subsides, lagoon appears, creating barrier reef

Volcano disappears, leaving behind coral atoll

ATOLL IN THE MAKING
An atoll is a ring of coral islands formed around a central lagoon. Charles Darwin (1809–82) thought atolls were formed by a reef growing around a volcanic island, which then subsided beneath the surface, a theory later proved to be correct.

Brittle skeleton of organ-pipe coral breaks easily

Branching, treelike skeleton

Queen scallops often make their home within the rose coral's folds

Living rose coral (not a true coral) can reach 20 in (50 cm) in diameter

ain coral gets its me from its nvoluted surface, ich looks like uman ain

ORGAN PIPES
Dull green tissue covers the bright red skeleton of living organ-pipe coral. Its anemone-like polyps emerge from each of the tiny pipes in the skeleton. Organ-pipe coral is not a true stony coral, but a relative of sea fans, soft coral, and sea pens.

A CORAL BY ANY OTHER NAME
Rose coral is a moss animal and grows in colonies on the seabed. Each colony is made up of millions of tiny animals, each living in one unit in its leaflike structure.

STONE BRAIN
ving brain coral's surface is covered with soft tissue. nemone-like polyps grow in rows along the channels n its skeleton. Brain corals are slow-growing stony corals, increasing in width a few inches each year.

BIGGEST AND BEST
This view of Australia's Great Barrier Reef shows fish feeding on plankton. The Great Barrier Reef, at 1,200 mi (2,000 km) long, is the largest structure in the world made by living organisms. Of the 350 kinds of coral, many spawn on the same night after a full moon, the water resembling an underwater snowstorm.

Mantle

A GIANT CLAM
The giant blue clam grows to about 1 ft (30 cm) long, but the largest giant clams may reach 3 ft 4 in (1 m). The colorful mantles exposed at the edge of their shells contain hordes of single-celled algae that make their own food by using the energy from sunlight. The clam gets some of its food by harvesting this growing crop of algae.

Life on a coral reef

CORAL REEFS HAVE an amazing variety of marine life, from teeming multitudes of brightly colored fish to giant clams wedged into rocks. Every bit of space on the reef provides a hiding place or shelter for some animal or plant. At night, a host of amazing creatures emerge from coral caves and crevices to feed. All the living organisms on the reef depend for their survival on the stony corals, which recycle the scarce nutrients from the clear, blue, tropical waters. People as well as animals rely on coral reefs, for they protect coastlines and attract tourist money. Some island nations even live on coral atolls. Sadly, in spite of being one of the great natural wonders of the world, coral reefs are now under threat. Reefs are being broken up for building materials, damaged by snorkelers and divers touching or stepping on them, dynamited by fishermen, ripped up by curio collectors, covered by soil eroded by the destruction of rain forests, and polluted by sewage and oil spills.

Green color helps camoufl... sea slug amon... seaweeds

Tentacles of sea anemone covered with stings to put off predators

Large eye for keeping a watch for danger

Layer of slimy mucus protects clown fish from anemone's stinging tentacles

Side fin used to steer and change direction

FRILLY LETTUCE
Sea slugs are related to sea snails but do not have shells. Many sea slugs living on coral reefs feed on corals, but the lettuce slug feeds on algae growing on the reef by sucking the sap from individual cells. Chloroplasts, the green part of plant cells, are then stored in the slug's digestive system, where they continue to trap energy fro... sunlight to make food. Many other reef sea slugs recycle the stings they eat from the coral's tentacles and are brightly colore... to warn that they are dangerous

Stripes brea... up clown fis... outline, so i... more difficu... for predator... to see the fis... on the reef

LIVING IN HARMONY
Clown fish, which shelter in anemones, live on coral reefs in the Pacific and Indian oceans. Unlike other fish, clown fish are not stung by the anemones. They are protected by a layer of slimy mucus, and the anemone's stinging cells are not even triggered by the fish's presence. Clown fish seldom venture far from their anemone home for fear of attack by other fish. There are many types of clown fish, some living only with certain kinds of anemones.

DATE MUSSEL
Many different clams live on coral reefs. This date mussel makes its home by producing chemicals to wear a hole in the hard coral. Like most clams, the mussel feeds by collecting food particles from water passing through its gills.

ate mussel on a coral
ef in the Red Sea

Narrow snout probes for sponges and other animals that grow on rocks

Bright colors help attract a mate

Plain yellow caudal (tail) fin

Adult

Adult emperor angelfish's colors and patterns act as signals to other angelfish

Special glands in skin make slug taste bad to deter predators

GROWING UP
Angelfish are common inhabitants of coral reefs. The young emperor angelfish looks quite different from the adult; possibly these colors protect it better. Once the adults pair up, they establish a territory on the reef where they can feed. Their colors and patterns help other emperors recognize them, and see that their patch of the reef is occupied.

Juvenile

Ring patterns may draw predator away from juvenile's more vulnerable head

Soft body has no shell to protect slug

NOTORIOUS STARFISH
The crown-of-thorns starfish devours the soft parts of a gorgonian coral. Like many other starfish, it feeds by turning its stomach inside out, producing enzymes that digest its prey. Plagues of these starfish attacked Australia's Great Barrier Reef in the 1960s and 1970s, killing many corals,

*t, slimy
t enables
g to crawl
er slippery
weed*

Bright green color from eating algae

Crown-of-thorns
starfish eating coral

Tentacles can be pulled back inside body for protection

Tentacles around mouth used for feeding

Spines on tough skin detract predators

Lettuce slug breathes through its skin, which looks like the leaf of a plant

One of five rows of tube feet helps sea cucumber crawl

COLORFUL CUCUMBER
One of the most colorful kinds of sea cucumber lives on or close to reefs in the Indo-Pacific region. Sea cucumbers are echinoderms (pp. 18–19), like starfish, sea urchins, and sea lilies. The sea cucumber puts out its sticky tentacles to feed on small particles of food. Once the food has stuck to the mucus on the tentacle, it is placed inside the mouth and the food removed.

Special fat tentacles for smelling food

Sea meadows

THE MOST ABUNDANT PLANTS IN THE OCEAN are too small to be
seen with the naked eye. Usually single-celled, these minute,
floating plants are called phytoplankton. Like all plants, they
need sunlight to grow, so are only found in the ocean's upper
zones. With the right conditions, phytoplankton multiply
quickly, within a few days, as each cell divides into two, and so
on. To grow, phytoplankton need nutrients from the seawater
and lots of sunlight. The most light occurs in the tropics but
nutrients there, especially nitrogen and phosphorus, are often
in short supply. Spectacular phytoplankton blooms are found
in cooler waters where nutrients (dead plant and animal waste)
are brought up from the bottom during storms, but also in both
cool and warm waters where there are upwellings of nutrient-
rich water. Phytoplankton are eaten by swarms of tiny, drifting
animals, called zooplankton, which provide a feast for small
fish, such as herring. Those in turn are eaten by larger fish,
such as dogfish, which are eaten by still larger fish or other
predators, such as dolphins. Some larger ocean animals
(whale sharks and blue whales) feed directly on zooplankton.

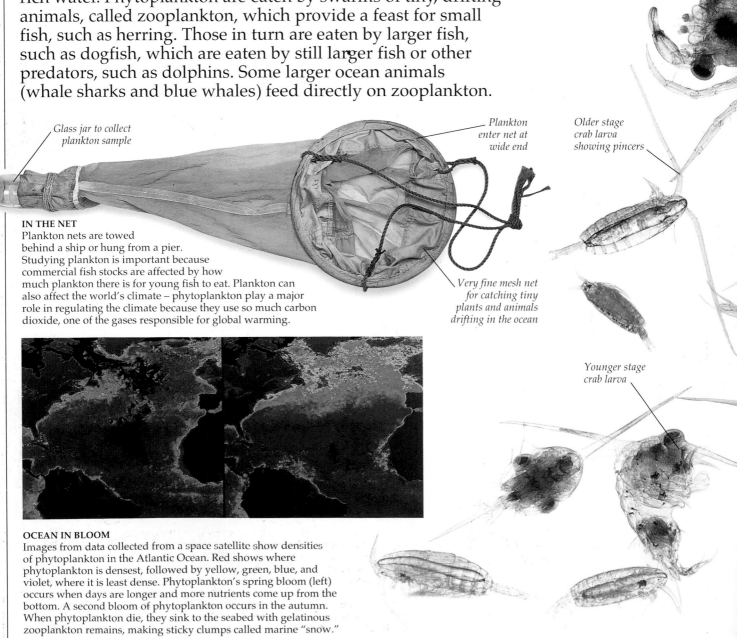

PLANT FOOD
This diatom is one of many phytoplankton that drift in the ocean.
Diatoms are the most common kind
of phytoplankton in
cooler waters, but
single-celled plants
called dinoflagellates
are common in tropical
waters. Many diatoms
are single cells, but this
one consists of a
chain of cells.

*Glass jar to collect
plankton sample*

*Plankton
enter net at
wide end*

*Older stage
crab larva
showing pincers*

IN THE NET
Plankton nets are towed
behind a ship or hung from a pier.
Studying plankton is important because
commercial fish stocks are affected by how
much plankton there is for young fish to eat. Plankton can
also affect the world's climate – phytoplankton play a major
role in regulating the climate because they use so much carbon
dioxide, one of the gases responsible for global warming.

*Very fine mesh net
for catching tiny
plants and animals
drifting in the ocean*

*Younger stage
crab larva*

OCEAN IN BLOOM
Images from data collected from a space satellite show densities
of phytoplankton in the Atlantic Ocean. Red shows where
phytoplankton is densest, followed by yellow, green, blue, and
violet, where it is least dense. Phytoplankton's spring bloom (left)
occurs when days are longer and more nutrients come up from the
bottom. A second bloom of phytoplankton occurs in the autumn.
When phytoplankton die, they sink to the seabed with gelatinous
zooplankton remains, making sticky clumps called marine "snow."

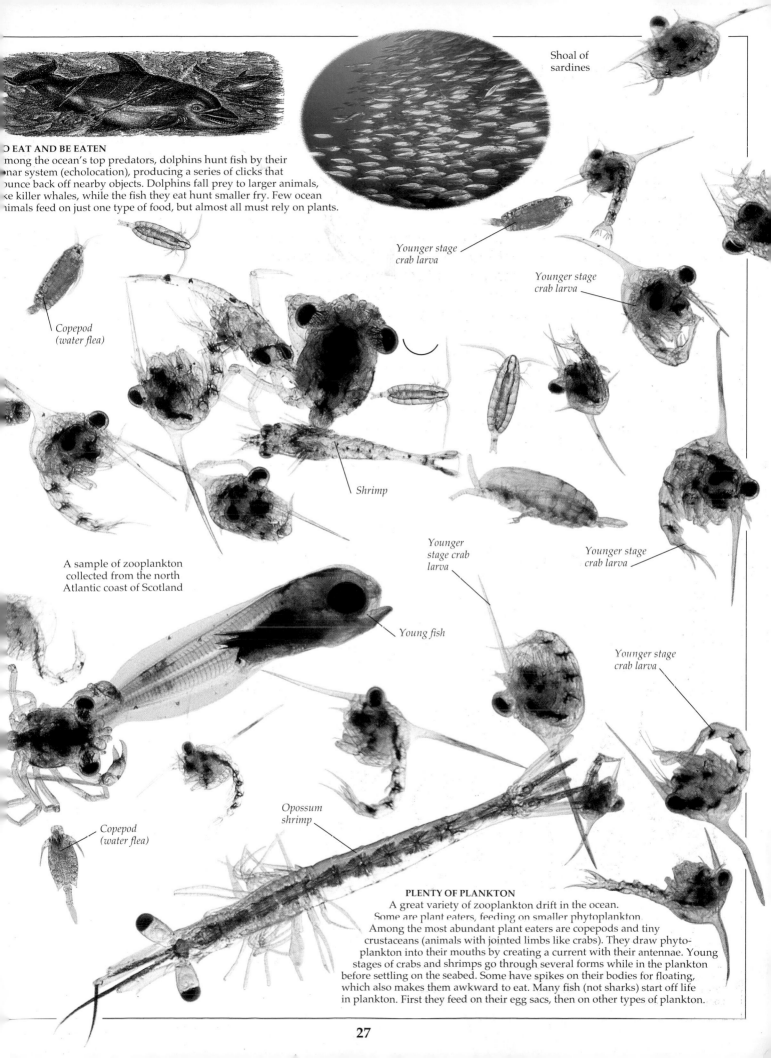

TO EAT AND BE EATEN

Among the ocean's top predators, dolphins hunt fish by their sonar system (echolocation), producing a series of clicks that bounce back off nearby objects. Dolphins fall prey to larger animals, like killer whales, while the fish they eat hunt smaller fry. Few ocean animals feed on just one type of food, but almost all must rely on plants.

Shoal of sardines

Younger stage crab larva

Younger stage crab larva

Copepod (water flea)

Shrimp

A sample of zooplankton collected from the north Atlantic coast of Scotland

Younger stage crab larva

Younger stage crab larva

Young fish

Younger stage crab larva

Copepod (water flea)

Opossum shrimp

PLENTY OF PLANKTON

A great variety of zooplankton drift in the ocean. Some are plant eaters, feeding on smaller phytoplankton. Among the most abundant plant eaters are copepods and tiny crustaceans (animals with jointed limbs like crabs). They draw phytoplankton into their mouths by creating a current with their antennae. Young stages of crabs and shrimps go through several forms while in the plankton before settling on the seabed. Some have spikes on their bodies for floating, which also makes them awkward to eat. Many fish (not sharks) start off life in plankton. First they feed on their egg sacs, then on other types of plankton.

Predators and prey

SOME OCEAN ANIMALS are herbivores (plant eaters), from fish nibbling seaweeds on coral reefs to dugongs chewing sea grasses. There are also many carnivores (meat eaters) in the ocean. Some, such as blue sharks and barracuda, are swift hunters, while others, such as anglerfish and sea anemones, set traps for their prey and wait with snapping jaws or stinging tentacles. Many animals, from the humble sea fan to the giant baleen whale, filter food out of the water. Sea birds find their meals in the ocean by diving for a beakful of prey. Other ocean animals are omnivores – they eat both plants and animals.

COOPERATIVE FEEDIN
Humpback whales herd schools of fish by letti out a stream of bubbles as they swim around With their mouths open wide to gulp in foo and water, whales ke the fish but expel wa through sieveli baleen plates their mouth

CAUGHT BY SLIME
Unlike the many jellyfish that trap prey with their stinging tentacles, common jellyfish catch small plankton (drifting animals) in sticky mucus (slime) produced by its bell. The four fleshy arms beneath the bell collect up the food-laden slime, and tiny, hairlike cilia channel it into the mouth.

Tiny prey caught in mucus

Dorsal fin runs along entire length of body

Crooked, yellow, fang-like teeth

Shorte pectoral fir

FANG FACE
The wolffish has strong, fanglike teeth for crunching through the hard shells of crabs, sea urchins, and mussels. As the front set are worn down each year, they are replaced by a new set growing in behind. Wolffish live in cool, deep, northern waters, where they lurk in rocky holes.

Tough, wrinkled skin helps protect wolffish living near the seabed

ines to
tect
chin

GRAZING AWAY
The European common sea urchin
grazes on seaweeds and animals
that grow on the surface of
seaweeds, such as sea mats.
The urchin uses the set of
rasping teeth, called
"Aristotle's lantern," on
the underside of its shell,
which are operated by a
complex set of jaws
inside. The grazing
activities of urchins
can control how much
seaweed grows in an
area. If too many
urchins are collected
for food or tourist
souvenirs, a rocky reef
can become overgrown
by seaweed.

Pelican
diving

*Brown
pelican
catches
fish in
pouch-
like beak*

*Tube feet used to
walk slowly along
the seabed*

*Sea urchin's mouth
surrounded by five
rasping teeth*

FISH FEED
Like all
pelicans, the
brown pelican has
a big beak with a
large flap of skin, or
pouch, to capture a
variety of fish. Once they
have spotted their prey, they
dive into the water, but are too
bulky to dive far below the
surface. Only brown pelicans dive
for their prey. When the pelican
surfaces, water is drained from the
pouch and the fish swallowed.

Tiny teeth of a
basking shark

TO BITE OR NOT TO BITE
A tiger shark's tooth is like a multipurpose tool, with a
sharp point for piercing prey and a serrated bladelike
edge for slicing. This shark can eat almost anything,
from hard-shelled turtles to soft-bodied seals and sea
birds. The rows of a basking shark's tiny
teeth are not used, since this shark
filters food out of the water with
a sieve of gill rakers.

TENTACLE TRAPS
The flowerlike dahlia anemones are deadly traps for
unwary shrimps and small fish that stray too close to
their stinging tentacles. When the prey brush past,
hundreds of nematocysts (stinging cells) are triggered
and fire their stings. These stings ensnare and weaken
prey. The tentacles pass the stricken
prey toward the mouth in the
center of the anemone – the
entrance to the baglike
stomach, where the
prey is digested.

*Stinging
tentacle*

Tiger
shark's
tooth

*Any undigested
pieces of food are
ejected through
the mouth*

*Suckerlike disk lets dahlia anemone
attach to any hard surface*

Homes and hiding

STAYING HIDDEN is one of the best means of defense – if a predator cannot see you, it cannot eat you! Many sea animals shelter among seaweeds, in rocky crevices, or under the sand. Matching the colors and even the texture of the background also helps sea creatures remain undetected. The sargassum fish even look like bits of seaweed. Hard shells are useful protection, at least from weak-jawed predators. Sea snails and clams make their own shells that cover the body. Crabs and lobsters have outer shells like suits of armor, covering the body and each jointed limb. The hermit crab is unusual because only the front part of the body and the legs are covered by a hard shell. Its abdomen is soft, so a hermit crab uses the empty shell of a sea snail to protect itself.

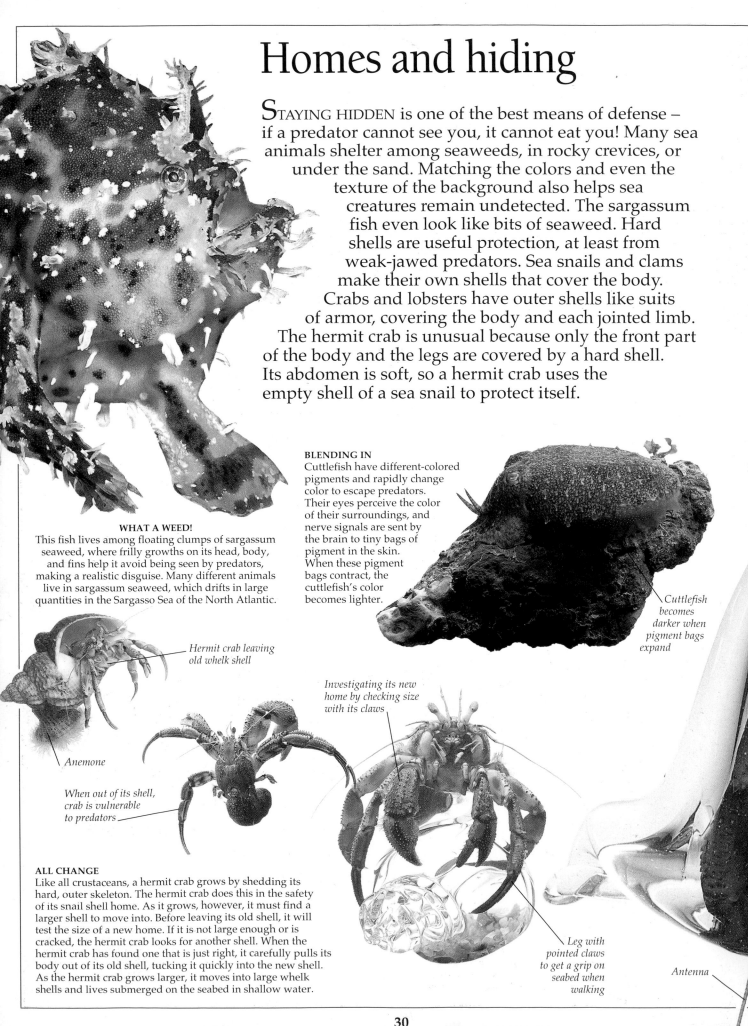

WHAT A WEED!
This fish lives among floating clumps of sargassum seaweed, where frilly growths on its head, body, and fins help it avoid being seen by predators, making a realistic disguise. Many different animals live in sargassum seaweed, which drifts in large quantities in the Sargasso Sea of the North Atlantic.

BLENDING IN
Cuttlefish have different-colored pigments and rapidly change color to escape predators. Their eyes perceive the color of their surroundings, and nerve signals are sent by the brain to tiny bags of pigment in the skin. When these pigment bags contract, the cuttlefish's color becomes lighter.

Cuttlefish becomes darker when pigment bags expand

Hermit crab leaving old whelk shell

Anemone

When out of its shell, crab is vulnerable to predators

Investigating its new home by checking size with its claws

ALL CHANGE
Like all crustaceans, a hermit crab grows by shedding its hard, outer skeleton. The hermit crab does this in the safety of its snail shell home. As it grows, however, it must find a larger shell to move into. Before leaving its old shell, it will test the size of a new home. If it is not large enough or is cracked, the hermit crab looks for another shell. When the hermit crab has found one that is just right, it carefully pulls its body out of its old shell, tucking it quickly into the new shell. As the hermit crab grows larger, it moves into large whelk shells and lives submerged on the seabed in shallow water.

Leg with pointed claws to get a grip on seabed when walking

Antenna

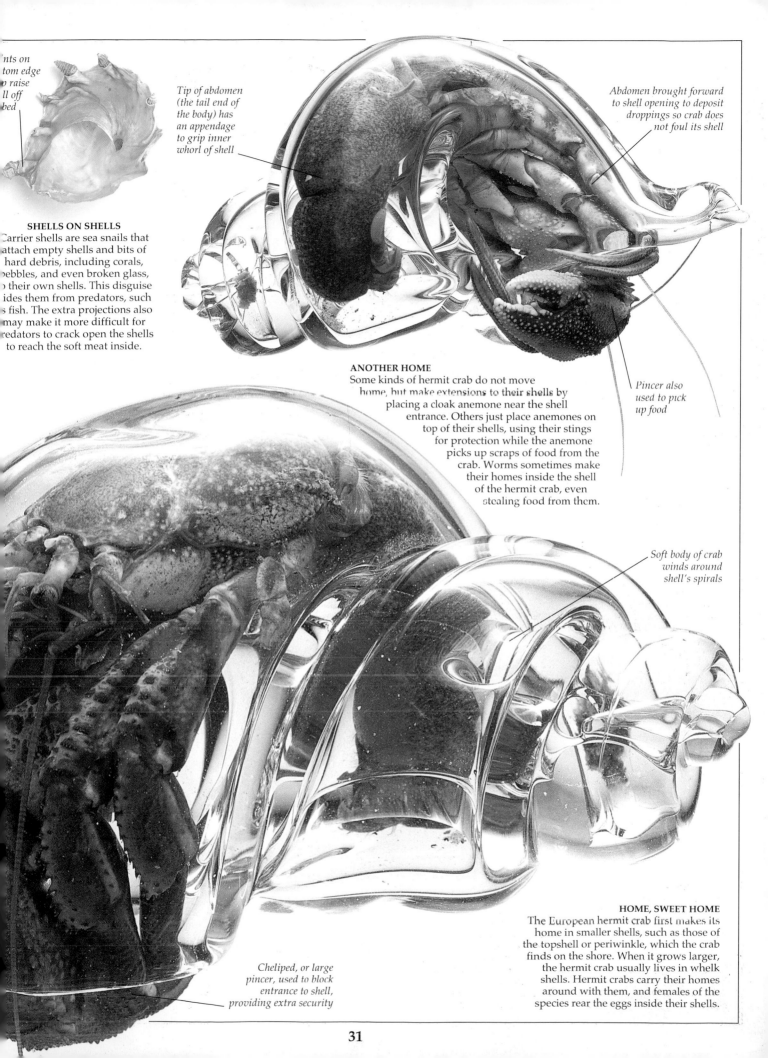

SHELLS ON SHELLS
Carrier shells are sea snails that attach empty shells and bits of hard debris, including corals, pebbles, and even broken glass, to their own shells. This disguise hides them from predators, such as fish. The extra projections also may make it more difficult for predators to crack open the shells to reach the soft meat inside.

*nts on
*tom edge
*o raise
*ll off
bed

Tip of abdomen (the tail end of the body) has an appendage to grip inner whorl of shell

Abdomen brought forward to shell opening to deposit droppings so crab does not foul its shell

Pincer also used to pick up food

ANOTHER HOME
Some kinds of hermit crab do not move home, but make extensions to their shells by placing a cloak anemone near the shell entrance. Others just place anemones on top of their shells, using their stings for protection while the anemone picks up scraps of food from the crab. Worms sometimes make their homes inside the shell of the hermit crab, even stealing food from them.

Soft body of crab winds around shell's spirals

Cheliped, or large pincer, used to block entrance to shell, providing extra security

HOME, SWEET HOME
The European hermit crab first makes its home in smaller shells, such as those of the topshell or periwinkle, which the crab finds on the shore. When it grows larger, the hermit crab usually lives in whelk shells. Hermit crabs carry their homes around with them, and females of the species rear the eggs inside their shells.

Attack and defense

MANY SEA CREATURES have special tactics for defending themselves from predators or attacking prey. Some produce venom (poison) to defend themselves and often advertise their danger with distinctive markings. Lionfish's stripes alert their enemies to their venomous spines, but being easy to see, they have to surprise their prey as they hunt in the open or ambush them from behind clumps of coral. Stonefish are also armed with venomous spines, blending perfectly with their background when waiting on a reef for prey to swim by. Octopi change color to match that of their background. If attacked, the blue-ringed octopus produces blue spots to warn that its bite is poisonous. Disappearing in a cloud of ink is another useful trick used by octopi, squid, and cuttlefish. Most clams withdraw their delicate soft parts into their shells, but the gaping file shell's tentacles are a deterrent – producing an irritating sticky fluid. But no defense method is foolproof. Even the most venomous jellyfish can be eaten by carnivorous turtles that are immune to their stings.

DEADLY STONEFISH
The stonefish is one of the deadliest creatures i the ocean. A stonefish' venom, which is project through the sharp spine on its back, causes such intense pain that a perso stepping on one may g into shock and die.

Ink cloud forming around cuttlefish

INK SCREEN
Cephalopods, which include cuttlefish, squid, and octopi, produce a cloud of ink when threatened, to confuse an enemy and allow time for escape. The ink, produced in a gland linked to the gut, is ejected in a blast of water from a tubelike funnel near its head.

Long, dorsal spine with venom glands in grooves

Horny projection above eye

Maerl (a chalky, red seaweed) grows in a thick mass along the stony seabed

Three venomous anal spines

BLUE FOR DANGER
If this octopus becomes irritated, or when it is feeding, blue-ringed spots appear on its skin, warning of its poisonous bite. Although this octopus is similar in size to a person's hand, its bite can sometimes be fatal. Blue-ringed octopi live in shallow waters around Australia and some Pacific Ocean islands.

KEEP CLEAR
The striped body of a lionfish warns predators that it is dangerous. A predator trying to bite a lionfish may be impaled by one or more of its poisonous spines. If it survives, the predator will remember the danger and leave the lionfish alone in future. Lionfish can swim openly, looking for smaller prey with little risk of attack. They live in tropical waters from the Indian to the Pacific oceans. In spite of being poisonous, they are popular aquarium fish because of their beauty.

Stripes warn predators that lionfish is dangerous

Two venomous spines on tail can pierce the swimmer's skin and inject its venom

Stingray's sting is sharp and serrated so it can easily pierce the skin

Painting of sea monsters, c. 1880s

Pectoral fin used for swimming

STING IN THE TAIL
This blue-spotted ray lives in the warm waters of both the Indian and Pacific oceans as well as the Red Sea, where it is often found lurking on the sandy seabed. If stepped on, shooting pains occur in the foot for over an hour, though the pain gradually wears off.

SOMETHING SCARY
Early sailors knew that some creatures living in the sea were dangerous and could kill people. Tales about these sea monsters, though common, often became greatly exaggerated. Monster stories were also invented to account for ships that foundered due to dangerous sea conditions.

When shell is closed, there is still a gap between the shell's two halves

VICIOUS JELLYFISH
Jellyfish are well known for their nasty stings, but none are nastier than those of the box jellyfish, or sea wasp. They often swim near the coasts of northern Australia and southeast Asia. Its stings produce horrible welts on anyone who comes in contact with their trailing tentacles. A badly stung person can die in four minutes.

Tentacles stick out when shell "gapes"

SHAGGY SHELLS
These gaping file shells cannot withdraw their masses of orange tentacles inside the two halves of their shell for protection, so the tentacles produce a sour tasting, sticky substance to deter predators. If tentacles are nibbled off, they can regrow. Gaping file shells make their homes in seaweed, putting out byssus threads for anchorage. They can also make "nests" among horse mussels and oarweeds. If dislodged from their homes, they can move by expelling water from their shell and using their tentacles like oars.

Shell is up to 1 in (2.54 cm) long

The jet set

ONE WAY TO GET AROUND QUICKLY in water is by jet propulsion. Squid, octopi, and some mollusks (like clams) do this by squirting water from the body cavity. Jet propulsion can be used just for swimming, but it also helps mollusks escape from predators. Squid are best at jet propulsion – their bodies are permanently streamlined to reduce drag (resistance to water). Some kinds of scallops also use jet propulsion and are among the few clams that can swim. Most clams (mollusks with shells in two halves) can only bury themselves in the sand, or are anchored to the seabed. The common octopus lives on the rocky seabed in the coastal waters of the Atlantic Ocean and the Mediterranean and Caribbean seas. If attacked, it can jet off.

TENTACLE TALES
A Norwegian story tells of Kraken, a giant sea monste that wrapped its arms arou ships before sinking them. T legend may be based on th mysterious giant squid, whi live in deep waters. Dead individuals sometimes are washed up on the shore, bi no one has ever seen them swimming in the depths.

JET PROPULSION
The engines powering jet planes produce jets of air to fly in much the same way that octopi, squid, and cuttlefish produce jets of water to propel themselves through the water.

Funnel

Long arms to grasp prey

FLEXIBLE FUNNEL
Sticking out from the edge of the octopus's baglike body is its funnel. The funnel can bend to aim the jet of water backward or forward, and so control the direction in which the octopus heads off.

Powerful suckers grip the rock, so octopus can pull itself along

1 ON THE BOTTOM
The common octopus hides during the day in rocky lair, coming ou night to look for suc food as crustacean The octopus slow approaches its pr then pounces, wrapping it between the webbing at the base of its arms

Sucke sensi to to and t.

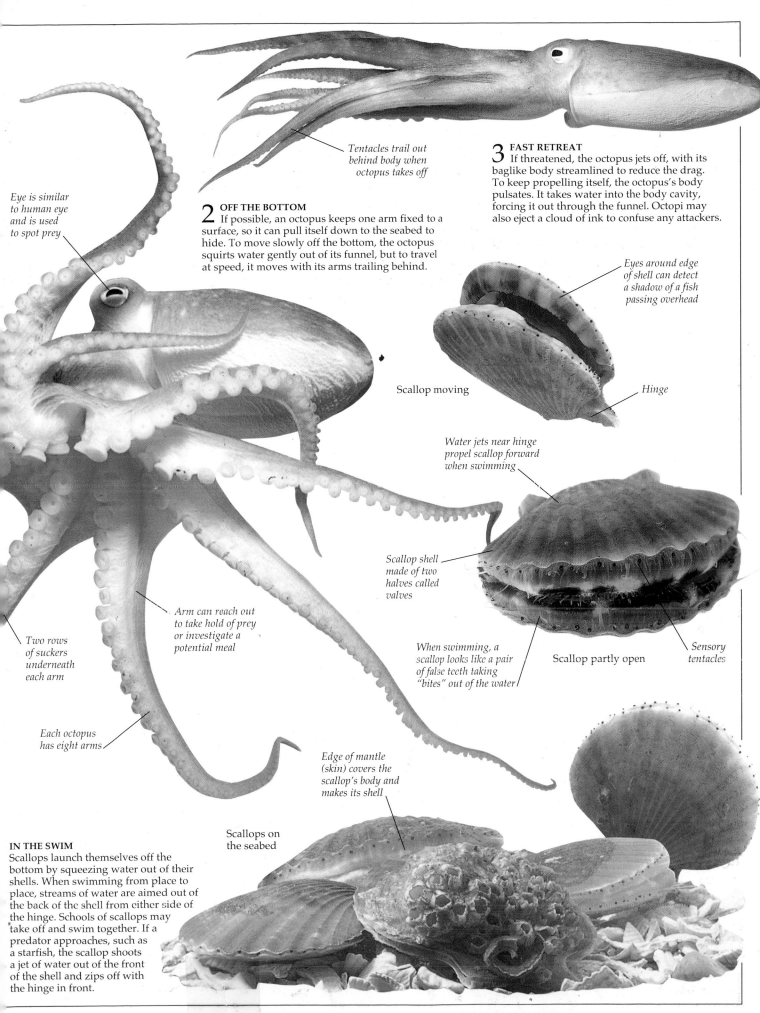

Eye is similar to human eye and is used to spot prey

Tentacles trail out behind body when octopus takes off

2 OFF THE BOTTOM
If possible, an octopus keeps one arm fixed to a surface, so it can pull itself down to the seabed to hide. To move slowly off the bottom, the octopus squirts water gently out of its funnel, but to travel at speed, it moves with its arms trailing behind.

3 FAST RETREAT
If threatened, the octopus jets off, with its baglike body streamlined to reduce the drag. To keep propelling itself, the octopus's body pulsates. It takes water into the body cavity, forcing it out through the funnel. Octopi may also eject a cloud of ink to confuse any attackers.

Eyes around edge of shell can detect a shadow of a fish passing overhead

Scallop moving

Hinge

Water jets near hinge propel scallop forward when swimming

Arm can reach out to take hold of prey or investigate a potential meal

Scallop shell made of two halves called valves

Two rows of suckers underneath each arm

When swimming, a scallop looks like a pair of false teeth taking "bites" out of the water

Scallop partly open

Sensory tentacles

Each octopus has eight arms

Edge of mantle (skin) covers the scallop's body and makes its shell

Scallops on the seabed

IN THE SWIM
Scallops launch themselves off the bottom by squeezing water out of their shells. When swimming from place to place, streams of water are aimed out of the back of the shell from either side of the hinge. Schools of scallops may take off and swim together. If a predator approaches, such as a starfish, the scallop shoots a jet of water out of the front of the shell and zips off with the hinge in front.

Moving along

FLYING FISH
Gathering speed underwater, flying fish leap clear of the surface to escape predators, then glide for over 30 seconds by spreading out the side fins.

AT SCHOOL
Fish often swim together in a school (like these blue-striped snappers), where a single fish has less chance of being attacked by a predator than when swimming on its own. The moving mass of individuals may confuse a predator; also, there are more pairs of eyes on the lookout for an attacker.

EVERY SWIMMER KNOWS that it is harder to move an arm or a leg through seawater than through air. This is because seawater is much denser than air. To be a fast swimmer like a dolphin, tuna, or sailfish, it helps to have a streamlined shape, like a torpedo, to reduce drag, or resistance to water. A smooth skin and few projections from the body also allow an animal to move through water more easily. The density of seawater does have an advantage in that it helps to support the weight of an animal's body. The heaviest animal that ever lived on earth is the blue whale, which weighs up to 150 tons. Some heavy-shelled creatures, like the chambered nautilus, have gas-filled floats to stop them from sinking. Some ocean animals, such as dolphins and flying fish, get up enough speed underwater to leap briefly into the air, but not all ocean animals are good swimmers. Many can only swim slowly, some drift along in the currents, crawl along the bottom, burrow in the sand, or stay put, anchored to the seabed.

IN THE SWING
During the day, many electric rays prefer to stay hidden on the sandy bottom, relying on their electric organs for defense, but they do swim if disturbed and at night when searching for prey. There are over 30 kinds of electric ray, mostly living in warm waters. Most other rays have spindly tails (unlike the electric ray's broad tail), and move through water using their pectoral fins. Waves pass from the front to the back of the pectoral fins, which, in larger rays like mantas, become so exaggerated that the fins actually beat up and down.

Electric ray's smooth skin can be either dark green or red-brown in color

Spiracle (a one-way valve) takes in water, which is pumped out through gill slits underneath

Electric rays can grow to 6 ft (1.8 m) and weigh as much as 110 lb (50 kg)

Swimming sequence of an electric ray, *Torpedo nobiliana*

Pelvic fin

DIVING DEEP
True seals move through water by beating their back flippers and tail from side to side and using their front flippers to steer. Their nostrils are closed to prevent water entering the airways. Harbor seals (right) can dive to 300 ft (90 m), but the champion seal diver is the Antarctic's Weddell seal, diving to 2,000 ft (600 m). Seals do not get the bends (pp. 48–49), because they breathe out before diving and, unlike humans, do not breathe compressed air. When underwater, seals use oxygen stored in the blood.

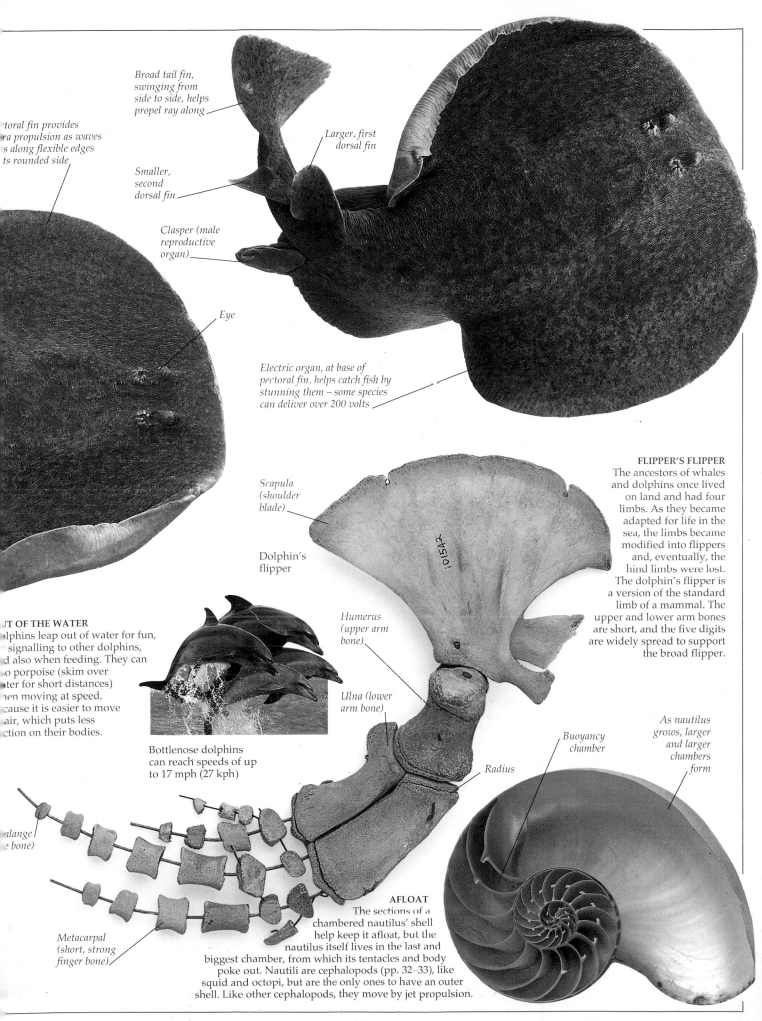

Broad tail fin, swinging from side to side, helps propel ray along

Larger, first dorsal fin

Smaller, second dorsal fin

...toral fin provides
...ra propulsion as waves
...s along flexible edges
...ts rounded side.

Clasper (male reproductive organ)

Eye

Electric organ, at base of pectoral fin, helps catch fish by stunning them – some species can deliver over 200 volts

Scapula (shoulder blade)

Dolphin's flipper

FLIPPER'S FLIPPER
The ancestors of whales and dolphins once lived on land and had four limbs. As they became adapted for life in the sea, the limbs became modified into flippers and, eventually, the hind limbs were lost. The dolphin's flipper is a version of the standard limb of a mammal. The upper and lower arm bones are short, and the five digits are widely spread to support the broad flipper.

...T OF THE WATER
...olphins leap out of water for fun,
...signalling to other dolphins,
...d also when feeding. They can
...o porpoise (skim over
...ter for short distances)
...en moving at speed,
...cause it is easier to move
...air, which puts less
...ction on their bodies.

Bottlenose dolphins can reach speeds of up to 17 mph (27 kph)

Humerus (upper arm bone)

Ulna (lower arm bone)

Radius

Buoyancy chamber

As nautilus grows, larger and larger chambers form

...alange
...e bone)

Metacarpal (short, strong finger bone)

AFLOAT
The sections of a chambered nautilus' shell help keep it afloat, but the nautilus itself lives in the last and biggest chamber, from which its tentacles and body poke out. Nautili are cephalopods (pp. 32–33), like squid and octopi, but are the only ones to have an outer shell. Like other cephalopods, they move by jet propulsion.

Ocean travelers

To make the most of the vast expanses of water, some sea animals travel great distances, crisscrossing the oceans to find the best places to feed and breed. Whales such as the humpback are well known for feeding in the cold, food-rich waters of the far north or south, traveling to the warm waters of the tropics to breed and give birth. Many long-distance voyagers, such as turtles, seals, and sea birds, feed out at sea, but come ashore to breed. Freshwater eels are unusual because they go to the ocean to breed, then their young travel back to rivers, where they grow to maturity. Salmon do the reverse, growing up in the ocean and returning to rivers to breed (pp. 56–57). Ocean travelers often make use of currents to speed them on their way. Even animals that cannot swim can travel far and wide by hitching a ride on another animal or by drifting along on a piece of wood.

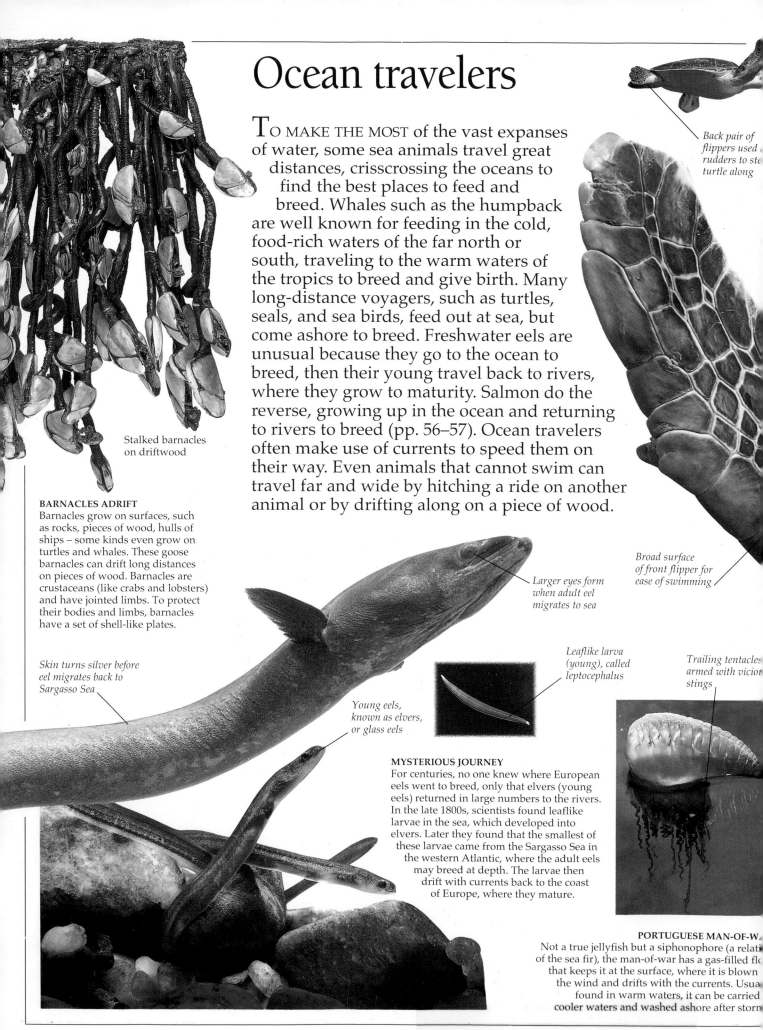

Back pair of flippers used as rudders to steer turtle along

Broad surface of front flipper for ease of swimming

Stalked barnacles on driftwood

BARNACLES ADRIFT
Barnacles grow on surfaces, such as rocks, pieces of wood, hulls of ships – some kinds even grow on turtles and whales. These goose barnacles can drift long distances on pieces of wood. Barnacles are crustaceans (like crabs and lobsters) and have jointed limbs. To protect their bodies and limbs, barnacles have a set of shell-like plates.

Skin turns silver before eel migrates back to Sargasso Sea

Larger eyes form when adult eel migrates to sea

Young eels, known as elvers, or glass eels

Leaflike larva (young), called leptocephalus

Trailing tentacles armed with vicious stings

MYSTERIOUS JOURNEY
For centuries, no one knew where European eels went to breed, only that elvers (young eels) returned in large numbers to the rivers. In the late 1800s, scientists found leaflike larvae in the sea, which developed into elvers. Later they found that the smallest of these larvae came from the Sargasso Sea in the western Atlantic, where the adult eels may breed at depth. The larvae then drift with currents back to the coast of Europe, where they mature.

PORTUGUESE MAN-OF-WAR
Not a true jellyfish but a siphonophore (a relative of the sea fir), the man-of-war has a gas-filled float that keeps it at the surface, where it is blown by the wind and drifts with the currents. Usually found in warm waters, it can be carried to cooler waters and washed ashore after storms.

Swimming sequence
of a green turtle

Turtle shell is
streamlined for
gliding through
water

UNDERWATER FLIER

Green turtles live in the warm waters of the Atlantic, Pacific,
and Indian oceans. Like all turtles, they come ashore to lay
their eggs. First the females mate in shallow water with the
waiting males. Later, under cover of darkness, the females
crawl up the beach to lay their eggs in the sand before
heading back to the water. They may return
several times in one breeding season to lay
further batches of eggs. Some green
turtles are known to travel several
hundred miles or more to reach
their breeding beaches where
they hatched themselves.
Green turtles feed on
sea grasses and
seaweeds.

Turtles are
air breathers,
and must come
to the surface to
breathe
through their
nostrils

Front pair of
flippers help
turtle to "fly"
through water

Green turtle
(*Chelonia mydas*)
is on the
endangered
species list

TURTLE TRIP

In the Japanese legend, Urashima Taro rides into the
kingdom of the sea on a turtle. After spending some time in
the depths, he begs the sea goddess to let him go home. She
allows this, but gives him a box that he must never open.
On his return he finds his home has changed and no one
knows him. Hoping for some comfort, he opens the box, but
the spell is broken. He becomes a very old man because
he has spent not three years – but 300 – in the sea.

The twilight zone

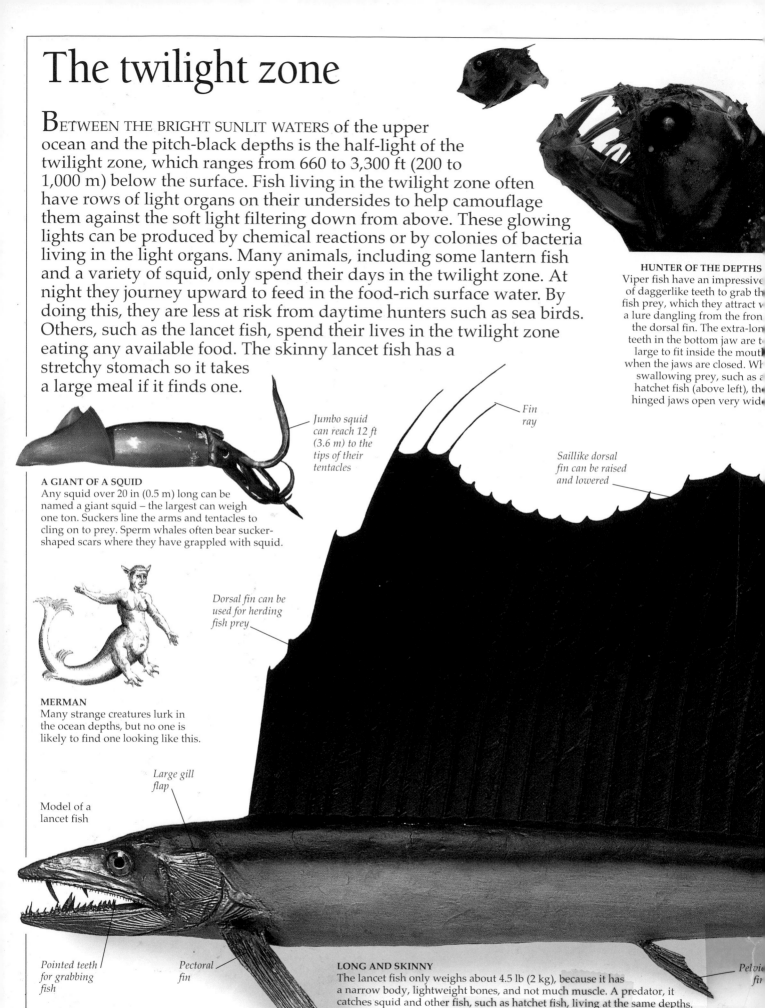

Bᴇᴛᴡᴇᴇɴ ᴛʜᴇ ʙʀɪɢʜᴛ sᴜɴʟɪᴛ ᴡᴀᴛᴇʀs of the upper ocean and the pitch-black depths is the half-light of the twilight zone, which ranges from 660 to 3,300 ft (200 to 1,000 m) below the surface. Fish living in the twilight zone often have rows of light organs on their undersides to help camouflage them against the soft light filtering down from above. These glowing lights can be produced by chemical reactions or by colonies of bacteria living in the light organs. Many animals, including some lantern fish and a variety of squid, only spend their days in the twilight zone. At night they journey upward to feed in the food-rich surface water. By doing this, they are less at risk from daytime hunters such as sea birds. Others, such as the lancet fish, spend their lives in the twilight zone eating any available food. The skinny lancet fish has a stretchy stomach so it takes a large meal if it finds one.

HUNTER OF THE DEPTHS
Viper fish have an impressive of daggerlike teeth to grab th fish prey, which they attract v a lure dangling from the fron the dorsal fin. The extra-lor teeth in the bottom jaw are t large to fit inside the mouth when the jaws are closed. Wh swallowing prey, such as a hatchet fish (above left), the hinged jaws open very wide

Jumbo squid can reach 12 ft (3.6 m) to the tips of their tentacles

Fin ray

Saillike dorsal fin can be raised and lowered

A GIANT OF A SQUID
Any squid over 20 in (0.5 m) long can be named a giant squid – the largest can weigh one ton. Suckers line the arms and tentacles to cling on to prey. Sperm whales often bear sucker-shaped scars where they have grappled with squid.

Dorsal fin can be used for herding fish prey

MERMAN
Many strange creatures lurk in the ocean depths, but no one is likely to find one looking like this.

Large gill flap

Model of a lancet fish

Pointed teeth for grabbing fish

Pectoral fin

LONG AND SKINNY
The lancet fish only weighs about 4.5 lb (2 kg), because it has a narrow body, lightweight bones, and not much muscle. A predator, it catches squid and other fish, such as hatchet fish, living at the same depths.

Pelvic fin

40

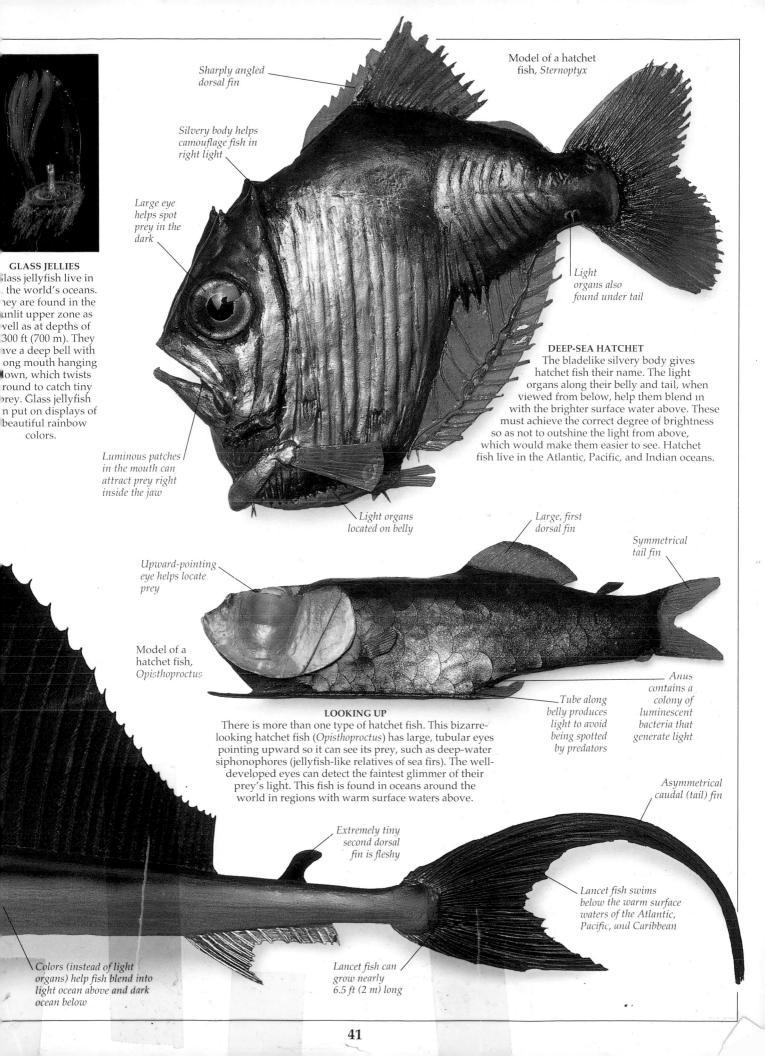

Sharply angled
dorsal fin

Model of a hatchet
fish, *Sternoptyx*

Silvery body helps
camouflage fish in
right light

Large eye
helps spot
prey in the
dark

*Light
organs also
found under tail*

GLASS JELLIES
Glass jellyfish live in
the world's oceans.
They are found in the
sunlit upper zone as
well as at depths of
2300 ft (700 m). They
have a deep bell with
long mouth hanging
down, which twists
round to catch tiny
prey. Glass jellyfish
can put on displays of
beautiful rainbow
colors.

DEEP-SEA HATCHET
The bladelike silvery body gives
hatchet fish their name. The light
organs along their belly and tail, when
viewed from below, help them blend in
with the brighter surface water above. These
must achieve the correct degree of brightness
so as not to outshine the light from above,
which would make them easier to see. Hatchet
fish live in the Atlantic, Pacific, and Indian oceans.

Luminous patches
in the mouth can
attract prey right
inside the jaw

Light organs
located on belly

Large, first
dorsal fin

Symmetrical
tail fin

Upward-pointing
eye helps locate
prey

Model of a
hatchet fish,
Opisthoproctus

Anus
contains a
colony of
luminescent
bacteria that
generate light

Tube along
belly produces
light to avoid
being spotted
by predators

LOOKING UP
There is more than one type of hatchet fish. This bizarre-
looking hatchet fish (*Opisthoproctus*) has large, tubular eyes
pointing upward so it can see its prey, such as deep-water
siphonophores (jellyfish-like relatives of sea firs). The well-
developed eyes can detect the faintest glimmer of their
prey's light. This fish is found in oceans around the
world in regions with warm surface waters above.

Asymmetrical
caudal (tail) fin

Extremely tiny
second dorsal
fin is fleshy

Lancet fish swims
below the warm surface
waters of the Atlantic,
Pacific, and Caribbean

Colors (instead of light
organs) help fish blend into
light ocean above and dark
ocean below

Lancet fish can
grow nearly
6.5 ft (2 m) long

The darkest depths

THERE IS NO LIGHT in the oceans below 3,300 ft (1,000 m), just inky blackness. Many fish in the dark zone are black too, making them almost invisible. Light organs are used to lure prey or communicate with a mate. Food is scarce in the cold, dark depths. All animals have to rely ultimately on what little drifts down from above. Deep-sea fish make the most of any available food by having huge mouths and stretchy stomachs, giving them a strange appearance. Often they are small or weigh little due to lightweight bones and muscles. Being lightweight helps fish in the dark zone maintain neutral buoyancy (keeping at one level without having to swim), even though most have no gas-filled swim bladders.

Lateral line organs sense vibrations in water made by moving prey

UMBRELLA MOUTH GULPER

With its large mouth opened wide, the gulper eel is always ready to swallow any food it may come across, such as shrimp and small fish. The gulper probably catches food by swimming along slowly with its mouth open. Adult gulper eels live in the lower part of the twilight zone and in the dark zone. Their young resemble the leaflike larvae of European eels (pp. 38–39) and are found in the sunlit zone from 330–660 ft (100–200 m). As they grow, the young gulper eels descend into deeper water.

Adults grow to about 30 in (75 cm) from head to tip of their long tails

Gulper eel, which lives in the dark depths below temperate and tropical surface waters

Tiny eye on end of nose

Long lower jaw

FISHING L[...]

The whipnose has a long whiplike lure [...] attracting prey. It is thought to use the lure [...] draw prey closer and closer to its mou[...] Unlike a true fishing line, [...] whipnose's nose does [...] have a hook on [...] end, so its p[...] must sw[...] toward[...] l[...]

Whipnose grows to 5 in (13 cm) in length

MONSTER MOVIES

Films about scary monsters are always popular, especially those from the pitch-black ocean depths. Curiously, so little of the deep ocean has been explored that there could be strange animals yet to be discovered. But most deep-sea animals are small, because there is so little food at these depths.

Model of a whipnose, which lives in the Atlantic and Pacific oceans

BINOCULAR EYES

Gigantura's extraordinary tubular eyes are probably used to pinpoint the glowing light organs of its prey. Even though *Gigantura* has a narrow body, its skin can stretch so that it can swallow fish larger than itself.

Lower lobe of tail fin longer than upper lobe

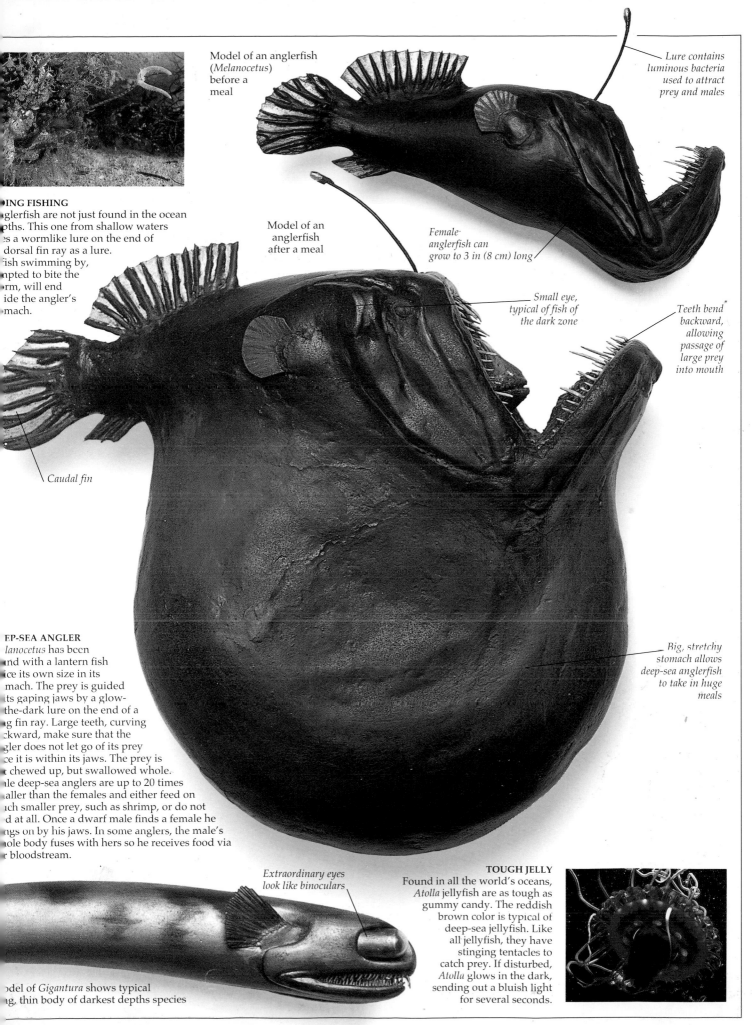

Model of an anglerfish
(*Melanocetus*)
before a
meal

Lure contains
luminous bacteria
used to attract
prey and males

Model of an
anglerfish
after a meal

Female
anglerfish can
grow to 3 in (8 cm) long

Small eye,
typical of fish of
the dark zone

Teeth bend
backward,
allowing
passage of
large prey
into mouth

Caudal fin

Big, stretchy
stomach allows
deep-sea anglerfish
to take in huge
meals

Extraordinary eyes
look like binoculars

[GOI]NG FISHING
[An]glerfish are not just found in the ocean
[de]pths. This one from shallow waters
[us]es a wormlike lure on the end of
[a] dorsal fin ray as a lure.
[A f]ish swimming by,
[te]mpted to bite the
[wo]rm, will end
[ins]ide the angler's
[sto]mach.

[DE]EP-SEA ANGLER
[*Me*]*lanocetus* has been
[fou]nd with a lantern fish
[twi]ce its own size in its
[sto]mach. The prey is guided
[to i]ts gaping jaws by a glow-
[in-]the-dark lure on the end of a
[lon]g fin ray. Large teeth, curving
[ba]ckward, make sure that the
[an]gler does not let go of its prey
[on]ce it is within its jaws. The prey is
[no]t chewed up, but swallowed whole.
[Ma]le deep-sea anglers are up to 20 times
[sm]aller than the females and either feed on
[mu]ch smaller prey, such as shrimp, or do not
[fee]d at all. Once a dwarf male finds a female he
[han]gs on by his jaws. In some anglers, the male's
[wh]ole body fuses with hers so he receives food via
[he]r bloodstream.

[Mo]del of *Gigantura* shows typical
[lon]g, thin body of darkest depths species

TOUGH JELLY
Found in all the world's oceans,
Atolla jellyfish are as tough as
gummy candy. The reddish
brown color is typical of
deep-sea jellyfish. Like
all jellyfish, they have
stinging tentacles to
catch prey. If disturbed,
Atolla glows in the dark,
sending out a bluish light
for several seconds.

On the bottom

THE BOTTOM OF THE DEEP OCEAN is not an easy place to live. There is little food and it is dark and cold. Much of the seabed is covered with soft clays or mudlike oozes made of skeletons of tiny sea animals and plants. The ooze on the vast open plains of the abyss can reach several hundred yards thick. Animals walking along the bottom have long legs to avoid stirring it up. Some grow anchored to the seabed and have long stems to keep their feeding structures clear of the ooze. Food particles can be filtered out of the water, for example, by the feathery arms of sea lilies or through the many pores in sponges. Some animals, such as sea cucumbers, manage to feed on the seabed by extracting food particles from the ooze. Food particles are the remains of dead animals (and their droppings) and plants that have sunk down from above. Occasionally a larger carcass reaches the bottom uneaten – a real bonanza for any mobile bottom dwellers, which home in on it from all around. Because food is scarce and temperatures so low, most animals living in the deep ocean take a long time to grow.

Underwater cables were laid across the Atla Ocean to relay telegraphic messages, c. 187

Dried remains of sea anemones

GLASSY STRANDS
This sponge grows anchored to the soft seabed by its stem of glass strands. Sea anemones often grow on their stems. When a glass-rope sponge dies, the cup-shaped part disappears and all that is left is the stem stuck in the seabed.

NOT A TRUE SPIDER
Sea spiders look like land spiders, but belong to a separate group called pycr gonids. Some deep-sea spiders have a leg span of 2 ft (60 cm) across, so can st along without stirring up clouds of particles. They can also swim, launching the seabed, bringing their legs toward their bodies, then sinking down agair

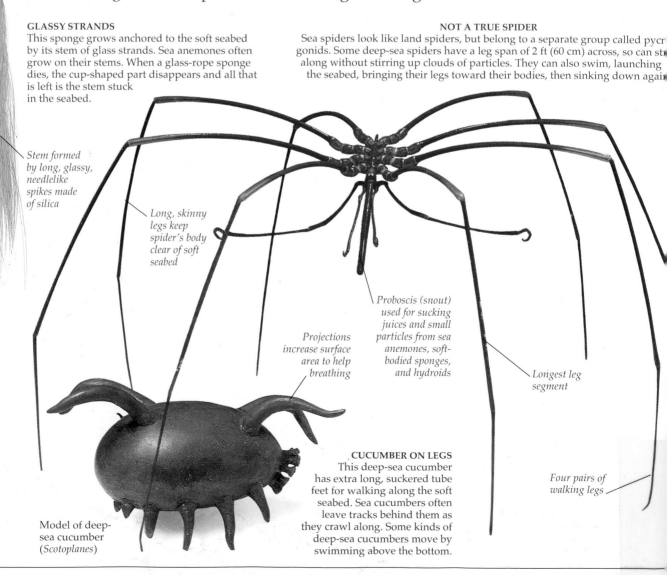

Stem formed by long, glassy, needlelike spikes made of silica

Long, skinny legs keep spider's body clear of soft seabed

Projections increase surface area to help breathing

Proboscis (snout) used for sucking juices and small particles from sea anemones, soft-bodied sponges, and hydroids

Longest leg segment

Four pairs of walking legs

CUCUMBER ON LEGS
This deep-sea cucumber has extra long, suckered tube feet for walking along the soft seabed. Sea cucumbers often leave tracks behind them as they crawl along. Some kinds of deep-sea cucumbers move by swimming above the bottom.

Model of deep-sea cucumber (*Scotoplanes*)

*cimens brought
from the deep
preserved by
·ing*

*Brittle star's arms,
wound around sea
pen for support*

LILY OF THE DEEP
Sea lilies use their
feathery arms to gather
food particles from the
water. Many kinds of sea
lily live on the floor of the
sea in trenches – from 330
to over 26,400 ft (100 to over
8,000 m) deep. Some have
roots and stems anchored to
the seabed, while those with
whorls of spikes (cirri) around
their stems can move using
their arms, dragging their
stems behind them. The spikes
along the stem act as props
and those at the base of the
stem can grip the seabed.

STARTING ON THE BOTTOM
Tsunamis are often called tidal waves, but they have nothing
to do with tides. They begin because of earthquakes or volcanoes
erupting on the seabed that send out shock waves through the water.
Traveling across the open sea at great speed, the waves are usually
less than 1 ft 8 in (0.5 m) high. Nearing the coast, they bunch up to
make towering walls of water that can devastate anything on land.

*Dried specimens
of deep-sea
brittle stars
(Asteronyxloveni)*

*Long arms
can grasp food
drifting by in
the water*

*Stem of sea
pen grows
up from
the seabed*

FLOWER BASKETS
The glassy skeletons
of Venus flower-
basket sponges have
long been admired
for their beauty. The
Japanese viewed them
as symbols of wedded
bliss, because pairs of
shrimp were often
found inside them. The
living sponge is not as
attractive, because it is
covered with soft
tissues. Most glass
sponges live in
deep waters, but
some live in
shallower
waters in
cold, polar
regions.

*Opening of
sponge covered
with sieve plate*

*Glassy
skeleton*

ALL IN THE ARMS
These deep-sea brittle
stars are usually
found wound around
sea pens on the ocean
floor. They use their
long, snakelike arms to
cling on to the sea pen
and to feed on small
creatures and other food
particles drifting by.
Climbing off the seabed
gives the brittle stars a
better chance to collect
food. Brittle stars and sea
pens are common bottom
dwellers, from shallow
water to deep seas in
oceans around the world.
These deep-sea brittle
stars are found between
depths of 330 5,940 ft
(100–1,800 m).

*Victorian
display of a
dried Venus
flower basket
(Euplectella
spergillium)*

Vents and smokers

IN PARTS OF THE OCEAN FLOOR, there are cracks in the crust from which extremely hot, mineral-rich water gushes. These vents (hot springs) exist at the spreading centers where the gigantic plates that make up the earth's crust are moving apart. Cold seawater sinks deep into cracks, where it heats up and collects quantities of dissolved minerals. At temperatures of up to 750°F (400°C), hot water spews out, depositing some minerals to form black smokers, or chimneys. Hot water produced by vents helps bacterial growth, which creates food from the hydrogen sulfide in the water. Extraordinary animals crowd around the cracks and rely on these microbes for food. Scientists using submersibles (pp. 50–51) in the late 1970s discovered the first vent communities in the Pacific. Since then, vents have been discovered in other spreading centers in the Pacific and the Mid-Atlantic Ridge.

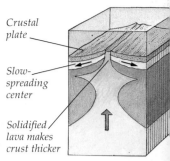

Crustal plate

Slow-spreading center

Solidified lava makes crust thicker

GROWING OCE
New areas of ocean floor continually being created spreading centers between t crustal plates. When lava (h molten rock) emerges from wit the crust, it cools and solidifi adding material to the edge each adjoining plate. Old ar of ocean floor are destroyed one plate slides under anoth Lava from volcanic eruption spreading centers can kill communities of vent anim

Animals cook if too close to the hot water in a vent

Plumes of hot water are rich in sulfides, which are poisonous to most animals

BLACK SMOKER
Animal life abounds in an active vent site, such as this one in the Mid-Atlantic Ridge. If the vent stops producing hot, sulfur-rich water, the community is doomed. Animals from dying vents must colonize a new site, which may be several hundred miles away across the cold, almost foodless bottom.

Dense numbers of animals crowd around a vent

predat nibble t off t wo

Giant clams in the eastern Pacific can grow to 12 in (30 cm) long

Some animals graze on mats of bacteria covering rocks near a vent

Model of vents found in the eastern Pacific

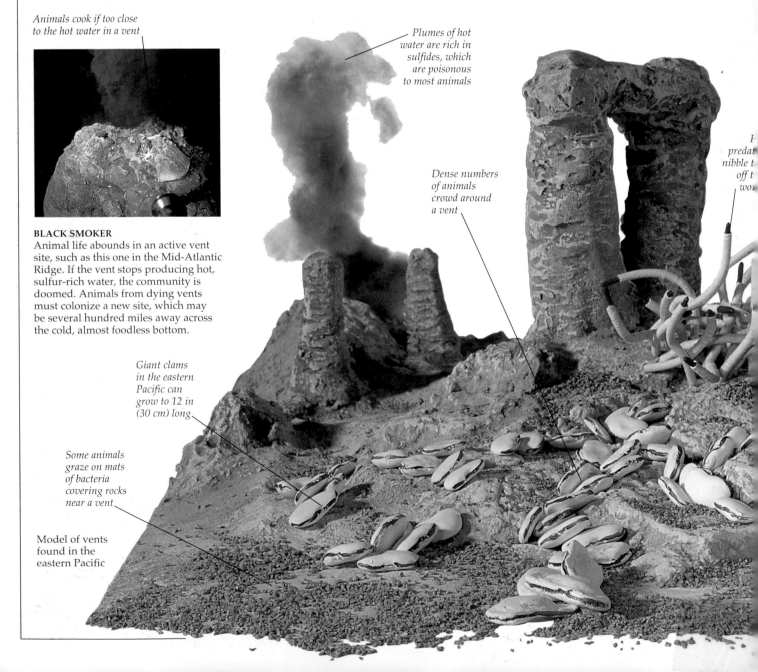

Deep-sea fish photographed from Alvin *near a vent on the Mid-Atlantic Ridge*

Alvin by the support ship, Atlantis II

Black smoker chimney can reach 33 ft (10 m) high

Chimney made from mineral deposits

CHAMPION SUBMERSIBLE
The U.S. submersible *Alvin* took the first scientists down to observe marine life near the Galápagos vents in the east Pacific in the 1970s. Since then, *Alvin* has completed many dives to vents around the world, to depths of 12,500 ft (3,800 m). Other submersibles that have dived on vent sites include the French *Nautile* (pp. 54–55) and the Russians *Mir I* and *II*.

VENT COMMUNITIES
This model shows the vent communities in the eastern Pacific, where giant clams and tube worms are the most distinctive animals. Vents in other parts of the world have different kinds of animals, such as the hairy snails from the Mariana Trench and eyeless shrimps from vents along the Mid-Atlantic Ridge.

Tube worm can grow to 10 ft (3 m) long

Giant tube worm has bacteria inside its body that provide the worm with food

Diverse divers

Umbilical supplies air, as well as electricity for light

Weight belt

PEOPLE HAVE ALWAYS WANTED to explore the sea, to look for sunken treasure, to salvage wrecks, to bring up marine products like pearls and sponges, or to examine the beautiful underwater world. More recently, underwater oil exploration and drilling have also required divers' skills. The first diving equipment were simple bells containing air and open at the bottom so the diver could work on the seabed. Later, diving suits with helmets were invented for divers to go deeper and stay down longer, with air pumped continually down a line from the surface. In the 1940s, the modern aqua-lung or scuba (*s*elf-*c*ontained *u*nderwater *b*reathing *a*pparatus) was invented. Divers could carry their own supply of compressed air in tanks on their backs.

Rope connecting bell to surface

Wooden bell

Weight

EARLY DIVING BELL
In 1690, Edmund Halley invented an open-bottomed divi bell, which could be resupplied with barrels of air lowere from the surface. Heavy weights anchored the bell to th seabed, and a leather tube connected the lead-lined air barrel to the wooden bell. Used at depths of 60 ft (18 m) the bell could house several divers at a time.

UNDERWATER WORKER
This diver, wearing a wet suit for warmth, has air pumped into the helmet via a line linked to the surface. A harness around the diver's middle carries tools. Flexible boots help the diver clamber around beneath an oil rig.

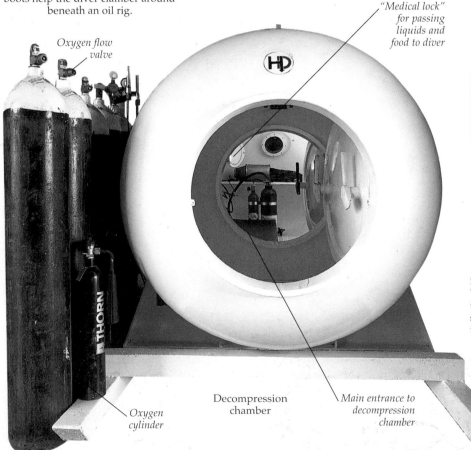

"Medical lock" for passing liquids and food to diver

Oxygen flow valve

Oxygen cylinder

Decompression chamber

Main entrance to decompression chamber

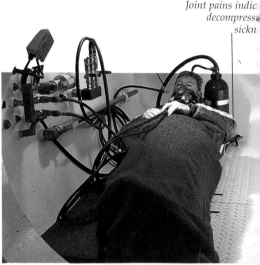

Joint pains indic decompress sickn

LIFE SAVER
When diving, the pressure on the body increases with the weight of water above. Air is supplied under the same pressure so the diver can breathe. Under more o this increased pressure, the nitrogen in the air supply contains 80 percent nitrogen) passes into the blood. If diver comes up too quickly after a long or deep dive the sudden release of pressure can cause nitrogen to form bubbles in the blood and tissues. This painfu sometimes fatal condition is called decompress sickness (the bends). The ailing diver is treate in a decompression chamber, its air pressur raised to the same pressure undergone during the dive. Pressure is then slowly reduced to normal pressure at the surface.

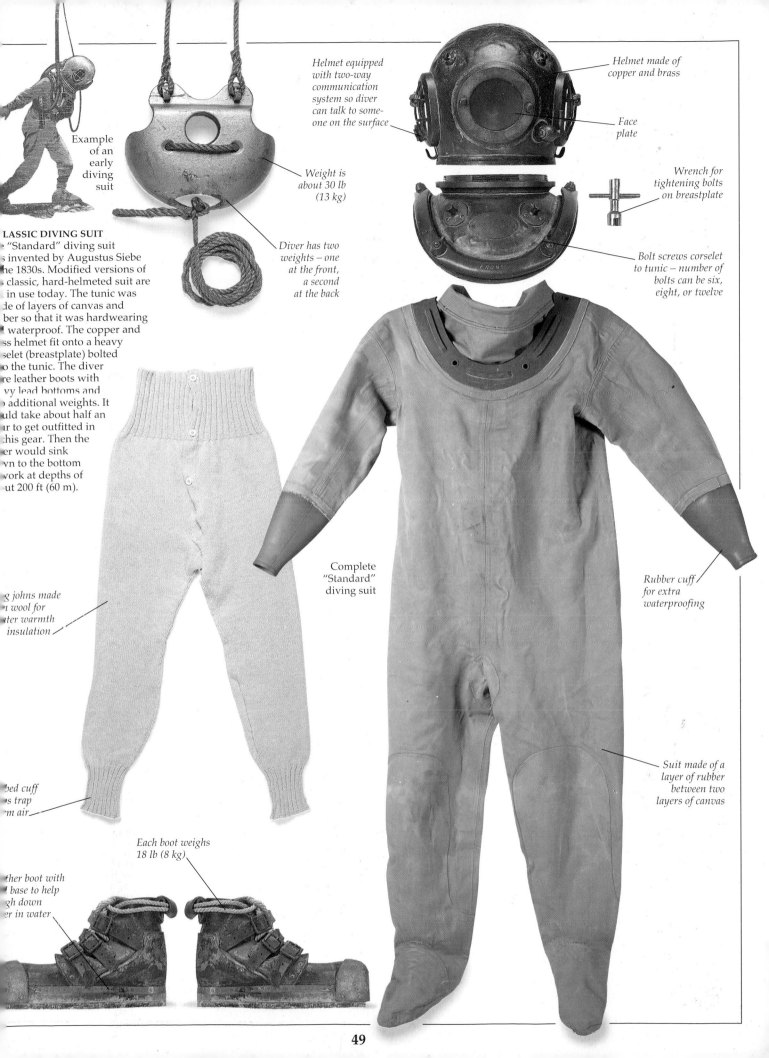

Example
of an
early
diving
suit

Helmet equipped
with two-way
communication
system so diver
can talk to some-
one on the surface

Helmet made of
copper and brass

Face
plate

Weight is
about 30 lb
(13 kg)

Wrench for
tightening bolts
on breastplate

Bolt screws corselet
to tunic – number of
bolts can be six,
eight, or twelve

Diver has two
weights – one
at the front,
a second
at the back

CLASSIC DIVING SUIT

e "Standard" diving suit
s invented by Augustus Siebe
he 1830s. Modified versions of
classic, hard-helmeted suit are
in use today. The tunic was
de of layers of canvas and
ber so that it was hardwearing
waterproof. The copper and
ss helmet fit onto a heavy
selet (breastplate) bolted
o the tunic. The diver
re leather boots with
vy lead bottoms and
additional weights. It
uld take about half an
r to get outfitted in
his gear. Then the
er would sink
vn to the bottom
work at depths of
ut 200 ft (60 m).

Complete
"Standard"
diving suit

Rubber cuff
for extra
waterproofing

Suit made of a
layer of rubber
between two
layers of canvas

g johns made
n wool for
ter warmth
insulation

bed cuff
s trap
m air

Each boot weighs
18 lb (8 kg)

ther boot with
base to help
gh down
er in water

Underwater machines

THE FIRST SUBMARINES had simple designs. They allowed travel underwater and were useful in wa More modern submarines were powered by diese or gasoline on the surface and used batteries underwater. In 1955, the first sub to run on nuclear fuel traversed the oceans. Nuclear power allowed submarines to travel great distances before needing to refuel. Today, submarines have sophisticated sonar systems for navigating underwater and pinpointing other vessels. They can carry high-powered torpedoes to fire at enem craft or nuclear missiles. Submersibles (miniature submarines), used to explore the deep-sea floor, cannot travel long distances. They need to be lowered from a support vessel on the surface.

Snort mast renews and expels air with help of bellows

Delayed action mine

Augur for drilling into enemy ship to attach mine on rope

Vertical propeller

Side propeller powered by foot pedals

"TURTLE" HERO
A one-man wooden submarine, the *Turtle*, was used during the Revolutionary War in 1776 to attach a delayed-action mine to an English ship blockading New York Harbor. The operator became disoriented when carbon dioxide built up inside the *Turtle*, and the mine struck metal instead of the ship's wooden hull. Both the ship and operator survived, but the mine was jettisoned.

UNDERWATER ADVENTURE
Inspired by the recent invention of modern submarines, this 1900 engraving depicted a scene in the year 2000 with people enjoying a journey in a submarine liner. In a way, the prediction has come true, as tourists can now take trips in small submarines to view marine life in places such as the Red Sea. However, most people explore the underwater world by learning to scuba-dive or snorkel.

External steering bar operated by diver

Internal steering position

Hand pump for pressurizing air reservoir and emptying ballast tanks

Front wheels smaller than back ones for easier turning

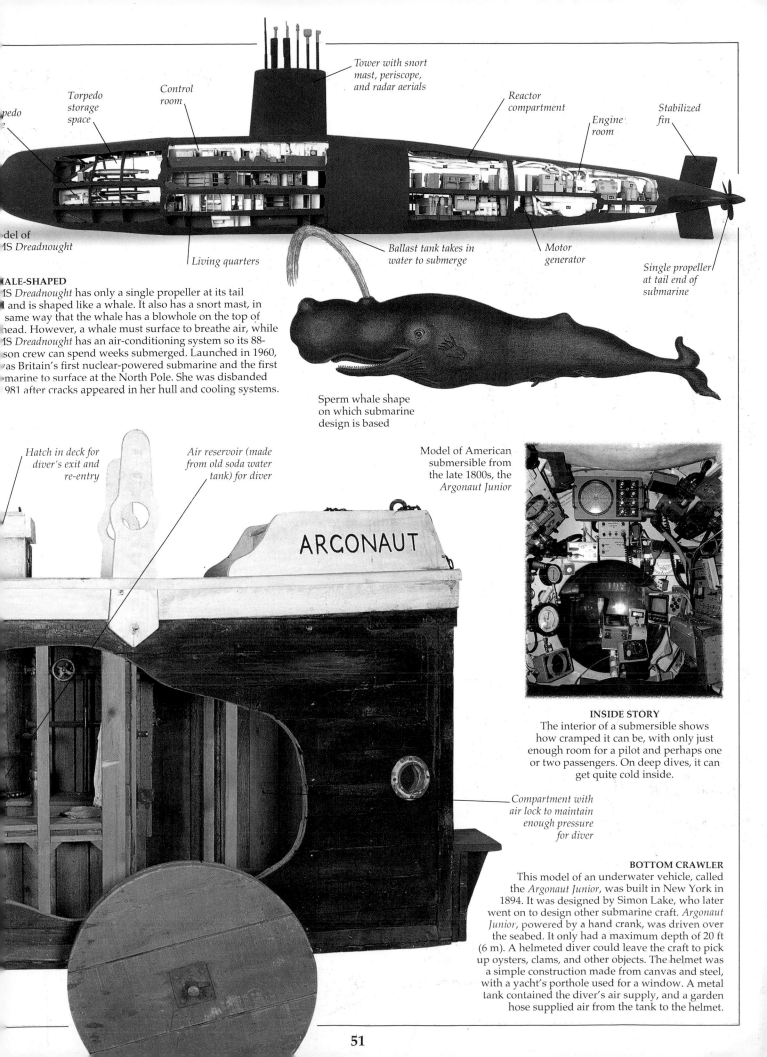

Tower with snort mast, periscope, and radar aerials

Torpedo storage space

Control room

...pedo ...2

Reactor compartment

Engine room

Stabilized fin

...del of ...MS Dreadnought

Living quarters

Ballast tank takes in water to submerge

Motor generator

Single propeller at tail end of submarine

...ALE-SHAPED
...MS *Dreadnought* has only a single propeller at its tail
... and is shaped like a whale. It also has a snort mast, in
... same way that the whale has a blowhole on the top of
...head. However, a whale must surface to breathe air, while
...MS *Dreadnought* has an air-conditioning system so its 88-
...son crew can spend weeks submerged. Launched in 1960,
...as Britain's first nuclear-powered submarine and the first
...marine to surface at the North Pole. She was disbanded
...981 after cracks appeared in her hull and cooling systems.

Sperm whale shape on which submarine design is based

Hatch in deck for diver's exit and re-entry

Air reservoir (made from old soda water tank) for diver

ARGONAUT

Model of American submersible from the late 1800s, the *Argonaut Junior*

INSIDE STORY
The interior of a submersible shows
how cramped it can be, with only just
enough room for a pilot and perhaps one
or two passengers. On deep dives, it can
get quite cold inside.

Compartment with air lock to maintain enough pressure for diver

BOTTOM CRAWLER
This model of an underwater vehicle, called
the *Argonaut Junior*, was built in New York in
1894. It was designed by Simon Lake, who later
went on to design other submarine craft. *Argonaut
Junior*, powered by a hand crank, was driven over
the seabed. It only had a maximum depth of 20 ft
(6 m). A helmeted diver could leave the craft to pick
up oysters, clams, and other objects. The helmet was
a simple construction made from canvas and steel,
with a yacht's porthole used for a window. A metal
tank contained the diver's air supply, and a garden
hose supplied air from the tank to the helmet.

Ocean explorers

W**ITH LITTLE TO SEE** on its surface, the ocean has always been a place of mystery. For centuries all that was known of marine life in the deep were creatures brought up in fishermen's nets or washed ashore. The first measurements of the oceans' depths were made by simply dropping a lead weight on a line until the operator felt it hit the bottom. The HMS *Challenger* 1870s expedition undertook deep-sea trawls, finally showing that the deep ocean was full of marine life. Echo sounders, invented during World War I, measured depths by bouncing single pulses of sound back from the seabed. This led to increasingly sophisticated sonar systems, such as GLORIA. Finally, the invention of manned submersibles allowed the deep-sea floor to be directly observed. In the last 20 years, startling new communities of animals have been found around hot springs on the ocean floor, while studies in shallow waters benefited greatly from the invention of scuba equipment (pp. 48–49). Yet despite all these modern methods, who knows what mysteries the ocean still holds – for much of it is yet to be explored.

Microscope used by a marine biologist in Scotland during the late 1800s

Engraving from 1900 of submarine bus in the year 20...

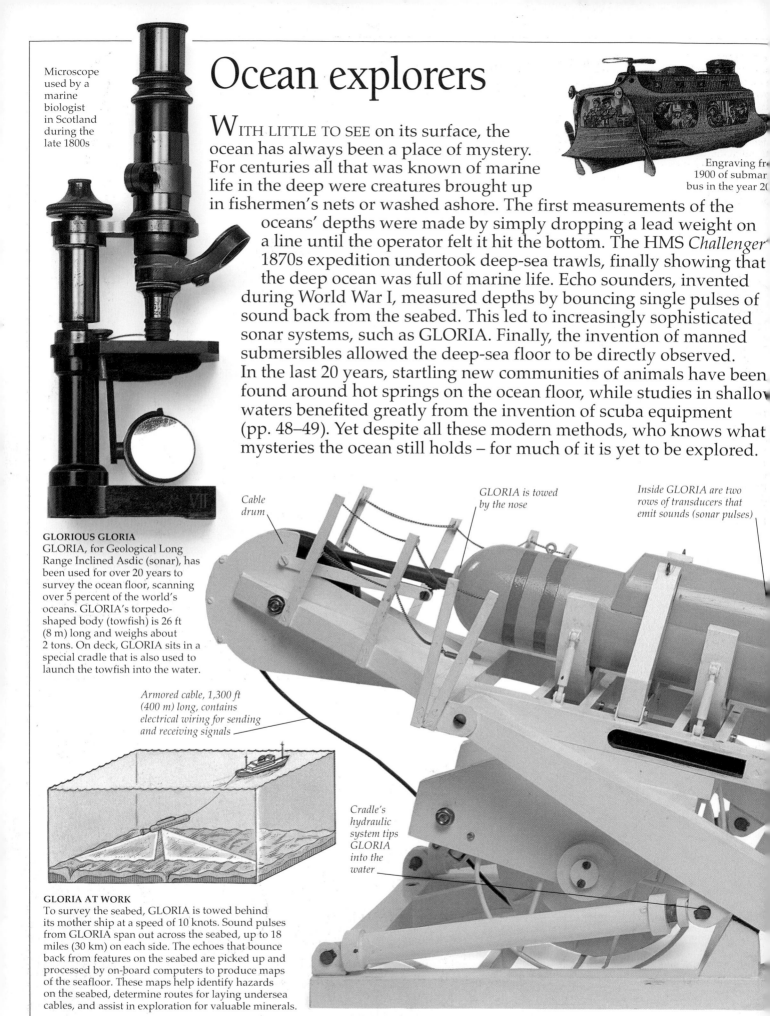

Cable drum

GLORIA is towed by the nose

Inside GLORIA are two rows of transducers that emit sounds (sonar pulses)

Armored cable, 1,300 ft (400 m) long, contains electrical wiring for sending and receiving signals

Cradle's hydraulic system tips GLORIA into the water

GLORIOUS GLORIA
GLORIA, for Geological Long Range Inclined Asdic (sonar), has been used for over 20 years to survey the ocean floor, scanning over 5 percent of the world's oceans. GLORIA's torpedo-shaped body (towfish) is 26 ft (8 m) long and weighs about 2 tons. On deck, GLORIA sits in a special cradle that is also used to launch the towfish into the water.

GLORIA AT WORK
To survey the seabed, GLORIA is towed behind its mother ship at a speed of 10 knots. Sound pulses from GLORIA span out across the seabed, up to 18 miles (30 km) on each side. The echoes that bounce back from features on the seabed are picked up and processed by on-board computers to produce maps of the seafloor. These maps help identify hazards on the seabed, determine routes for laying undersea cables, and assist in exploration for valuable minerals.

SNORKELING

[S]imple way to observe [life] underwater is to [sno]rkel. The snorkel [goe]s under the strap [on t]he face mask and [stic]ks out above the [wat]er. By breathing [in t]hrough the mouth-[piec]e, air is drawn down [the] snorkel, and air is [exp]elled through the [sno]rkel by breathing out.

Diver looking at grouper fish in the Red Sea

Face mask traps air to let swimmer view life in the water

Air expelled through end of snorkel

Flippers propel swimmer along, but arms should be kept near the body for streamlining

Swimmer breathes in air and expels it out through mouthpiece

Snorkel tube

SCUBA DIVING

[Th]e of scuba equipment has proved [inv]aluable in the study of marine [life] in shallow waters. Instead of [bri]nging animals into an aquarium, [ma]rine biologists can observe them [in t]he wild. However, some animals, [suc]h as hammerhead sharks, are [sen]sitive to the noises made by air [bub]bles and may be scared away.

Flippers used in snorkeling and scuba diving

Rope guide, used during recovery of GLORIA

Deep Star can reach depths of 4,000 ft (1,200 m)

DEEP STARS
Many different submersibles have been used for underwater exploration (left). The deepest dive ever made was to 36,000 ft (10,911 m) in the Mariana Trench by the Swiss scientist Jacques Piccard (1922—) in the U.S. navy's bathyscaphe, *Trieste*, in 1960. The dive down took 4 hours and 48 minutes.

GLORIA covers 7,700 sq mi (20,000 sq km) in a day

Launching cradle weighs about 13 tons

Wrecks on the seabed

EVER SINCE PEOPLE TOOK TO THE SEA in boats, there have been wrecks on the seabed. Drifts of mud and sand cover them, preserving wooden boats for centuries. This sediment protects the timbers from wood-boring animals by keeping out the oxygen they need. Seawater, however, badly corrodes metal-hulled ships. The *Titanic*'s steel hull could disintegrate within a hundred years. Wrecks in shallow water get covered by plant and animal life and turn into living reefs. Animals such as corals and sponges grow on the outside of the ship, while fish use the inside as an underwater cave to shelter in. Wrecks and their contents tell much about life in the past, but first archeologists must survey them carefully. Objects brought up must be washed clean of salt or preserved with chemicals. Treasure seekers, unfortunately, can do much damage.

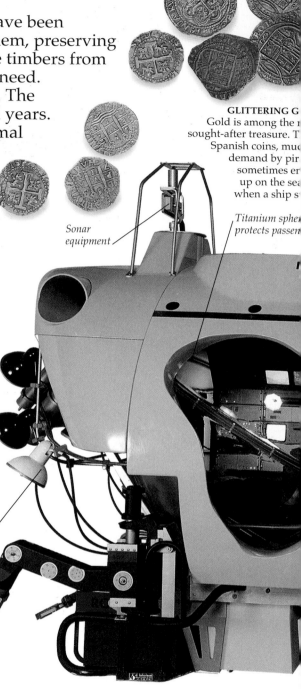

Less valuable silver coin

GLITTERING G
Gold is among the r sought-after treasure. T Spanish coins, muc demand by pir sometimes er up on the se when a ship s

Sonar equipment

Titanium sphe protects passen

SUPER SUB
The French submersible *Nautile* recovered objects from the seabed surrounding the wreck of the *Titanic*. When the ship went down, it broke in two, scattering objects far and wide. Only a submersible could dive deep enough to reach the *Titanic*, 2.3 mi (3,780 m) down. A sphere made of titanium metal to withstand the immense pressure at these depths, the *Nautile* has space for only three – a pilot, a co-pilot, and an observer. Extra-thick, curved Plexiglas portholes flatten on the dive due to pressure. The journey to the wreck takes about an hour and a half, and *Nautile* can stay down for eight hours.

Lights for video camera

VALUABLE PROPERTY
In 1892, divers worked on the wreck of the tug *L'Abeille*, which sank off Le Havre, France. For centuries, people have salvaged wrecks to bring up items of value.

Manipulator arm for picking objects off seabed

SAD REMINDERS
Many items recovered from the *Titanic* wreck were not valuable but everyday items used by those aboard. Personal effects, such as buttons or just cutlery, remind us of those who died.

THE UNSINKABLE SHIP
In 1912, the *Titanic* sailed from England to New York on her maiden voyage. Because of her hull's water-tight compartments, she was thought unsinkable, but hit an iceberg four days into the voyage. She took two hours and forty minutes to sink, with only 705 people saved of 2,228. She was discovered in 1985 by a French-U.S. team using remote-controlled video equipment. Submersibles *Alvin* (United States) and *Mir* (Russia) have also dived to the wreck since then.

PLANE WRECK
Airplanes sometimes crash into the sea and sink to the bottom, like this Japanese biplane discovered off Papua New Guinea in the Pacific. The Bermuda Triangle, an area in the Atlantic, is famous for the many planes and ships that mysteriously disappeared there.

SUNKEN TREASURE
These precious jewels are among many valuable items salvaged from the wreck of a Spanish galleon, the *Tolossa*, in the 1970s. Bound for Mexico in 1724, a hurricane blew up and it foundered on a massive coral reef. Many luxury goods were recovered from the wreck, which show that the Spanish were exporting fine things to their New World colonies during the 1700s. Other items from the wreck include brass guns, iron grenades, and hundreds of pearls.

Gold, diamonds, and pearls salvaged from the wreck of the Tolossa off Hispaniola

Nautile *measures 26 ft 3 in (8 m) in length*

Thruster provides the power for the 3.7 mi (6 km) dive

NAUTILE

IFREMER

Encrusted Roman jar

Barnacle

Mollusk

MISSING LAND
This poster advertises a film about the lost continent of Atlantis, which supposedly sank beneath the sea. This myth may be true, since a Greek island sank beneath the waves after an earthquake in 1450 B.C.

HOME, SWEET HOME
Hard barnacle shells and tubes of worms grew on this Roman jar while it rested for hundreds of years on the seabed. Animals that normally live on rocks are just as happy to settle on any hard objects left in the sea, such as shipwrecks, but some animal growths are hard to remove without damaging objects.

Worm tube

Harvesting fish

FISH ARE THE MOST popular kind of seafood, with some 70 million tons caught around the world each year. Some fish are caught by hand-thrown nets and traps in local waters, but far more are caught at sea by modern fishing vessels using the latest technology. Some fish are caught on long lines with many hooks or ensnared when they swim into long walls of drift nets. Bottom-dwelling fish are trawled or whole schools are gathered up in huge nets set in midwater. The use of sonar to detect schools leaves few places where fish can escape notice. Even fish living in deep waters, such as orange roughy at depths of 3,300 ft (1,000 m), can be brought up in numbers. Many people are concerned that too many fish are being caught and numbers will take a long time to recover. Competition for fish stocks is fierce and it is difficult for fishermen to make a living. But some fish, like salmon, are grown in farms to help meet demands.

1 HATCHING OUT
Salmon begin life in rivers and streams, where they hatch from eggs laid in a shallow hollow among gravel. First the fry (alevins) grow, using the contents of their egg sac attached to their bellies as food.

2 YOUNG SALMON
At a few weeks old, the egg sac disappears, so young salmon must feed on tiny insects in the river. Soon dark spots appear on the parr (young salmon). The parr stay in the river for a year or more before turning into silvery smolt that head for the sea.

3 AT SEA
Atlantic salmon spend up to four years at sea, feeding on other fish. They grow rapidly, putting on several pounds (or kilos) annually. Then the mature salmon return to their home rivers and streams, where they hatch. They recognize their home stream by a number of clues, including its "smell" – combinations of tiny quantities of substances in the water.

Fin rays are well developed

Large, first dorsal fin

Pelvic fin

Pectoral fin

Operculum (flap covering gills)

Mouth for feeding and taking in water to "breathe".

FISH FARMING
Salmon are among the few kinds of sea fish to be farmed successfully. Young salmon are reared in fresh water. When they are large enough, they are released into floating pens in the sea. These are located in relatively calm waters so the fish are not washed away. To help them grow quickly, the salmon are fed regularly with dried fish pellets. Like any farmed animals, care must be taken to keep the salmon from developing diseases.

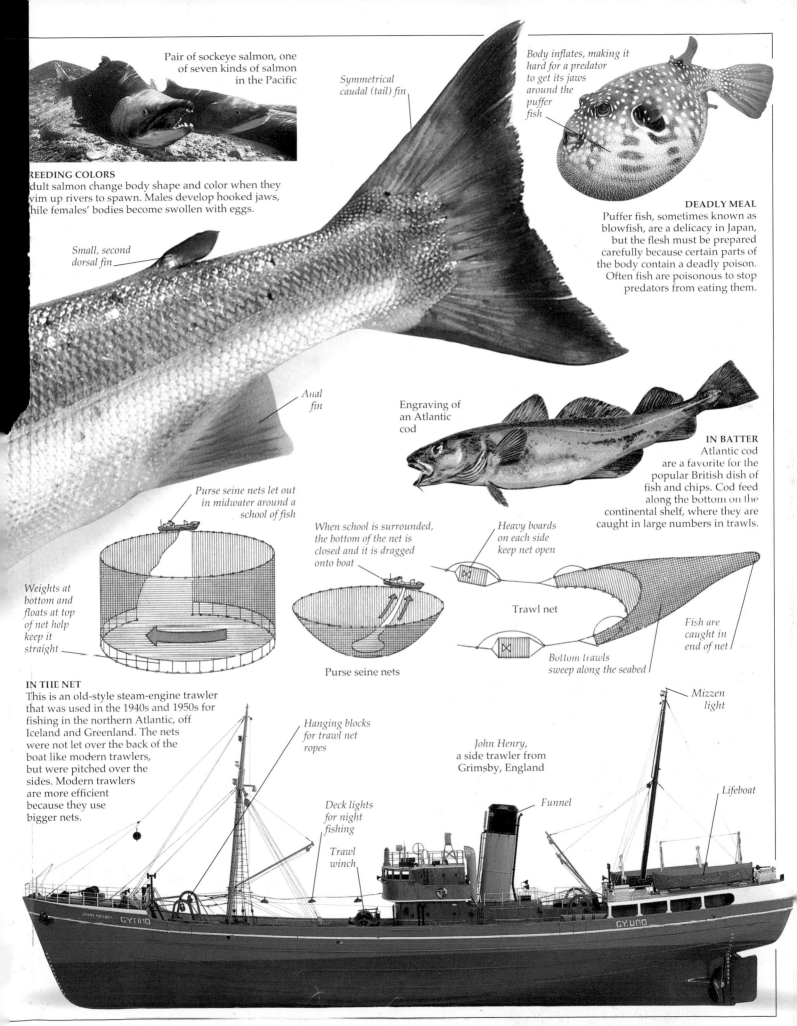

Pair of sockeye salmon, one of seven kinds of salmon in the Pacific

Symmetrical caudal (tail) fin

Body inflates, making it hard for a predator to get its jaws around the puffer fish

BREEDING COLORS
Adult salmon change body shape and color when they swim up rivers to spawn. Males develop hooked jaws, while females' bodies become swollen with eggs.

DEADLY MEAL
Puffer fish, sometimes known as blowfish, are a delicacy in Japan, but the flesh must be prepared carefully because certain parts of the body contain a deadly poison. Often fish are poisonous to stop predators from eating them.

Small, second dorsal fin

Anal fin

Engraving of an Atlantic cod

IN BATTER
Atlantic cod are a favorite for the popular British dish of fish and chips. Cod feed along the bottom on the continental shelf, where they are caught in large numbers in trawls.

Purse seine nets let out in midwater around a school of fish

When school is surrounded, the bottom of the net is closed and it is dragged onto boat

Heavy boards on each side keep net open

Weights at bottom and floats at top of net help keep it straight

Trawl net

Fish are caught in end of net

Purse seine nets

Bottom trawls sweep along the seabed

IN THE NET
This is an old-style steam-engine trawler that was used in the 1940s and 1950s for fishing in the northern Atlantic, off Iceland and Greenland. The nets were not let out over the back of the boat like modern trawlers, but were pitched over the sides. Modern trawlers are more efficient because they use bigger nets.

Mizzen light

Hanging blocks for trawl net ropes

John Henry, a side trawler from Grimsby, England

Lifeboat

Deck lights for night fishing

Funnel

Trawl winch

Ocean products

PEOPLE HAVE ALWAYS HARVESTED plants and animals from the ocean. Many different kinds are collected for food, from fish, crustaceans (shrimp, lobsters), mollusks (clams, squid) to more unusual foods such as sea cucumbers, barnacles, and jellyfish. Seaweeds also are eaten, either in a recognizable state or as an ingredient of ice cream and other processed foods. The products made from sea creatures are amazing, although many (such as mother-of-pearl buttons and sponges) are now made with synthetic materials. Yet the appeal of natural ocean products is so great that some animals and seaweeds are grown in farms. Among the sea creatures cultivated today are sponges, giant clams (for their pretty shells), mussels (for food), and pearl oysters. Farming is one way to meet product demand, and to avoid over-harvesting the ocean's wildlife.

Yarn dyed purple from pigment of sea snails

ROYAL PURPLE
Sea snails were used to make purple dye for clothes worn by kings in ancient times. Making dye was a smelly business, as huge quantities of salted snails were left in vats gouged out of rock. The purple liquid was collected and heated to concentrate the dye. These sea snails (from Florida and the Caribbean) are used to make purple dye.

Slate-pencil sea urchin from tropical coral reefs in the Indo-Pacific

Short, blunt spines surround mouth

Long, very strong spines help protect urchin from predators

Five strong white teeth protrude from urchin's mouth (viewed from underneath)

Soft skeleton is all that is left after processing living sponge

USEFUL SPINES
The spines of this urchin were once used as pencils to write on slate boards. Slate-pencil urchins are still collected, their spines used for wind chimes. The spines, hung from threads, clink together when the wind blows through them. Urchins use their big spines to help them walk across the seabed when they emerge from crevices to feed at night.

Spines help urchin move and stay in place

SOFT SKELETON
Bath sponges grow among sea grasses in reef lagoons. When harvested from the bottom, the sponges are covered with slimy, living tissues. Collected from the Mediterranean, Caribbean, and Pacific, natural sponges are prone to diseases and over-collecting.

SEAWEED FARM
In Japan, seaweeds are used in crackers or to wrap up bites of raw fish. Nori, a red seaweed, is grown in the sea on bamboo poles, collected, and dried. Laver, another red seaweed, is eaten in Wales, in the U.K. Agar, a jelly-like substance, is made from red seaweeds and used in foods and in medical research. Seaweeds are also used in fertilizers.

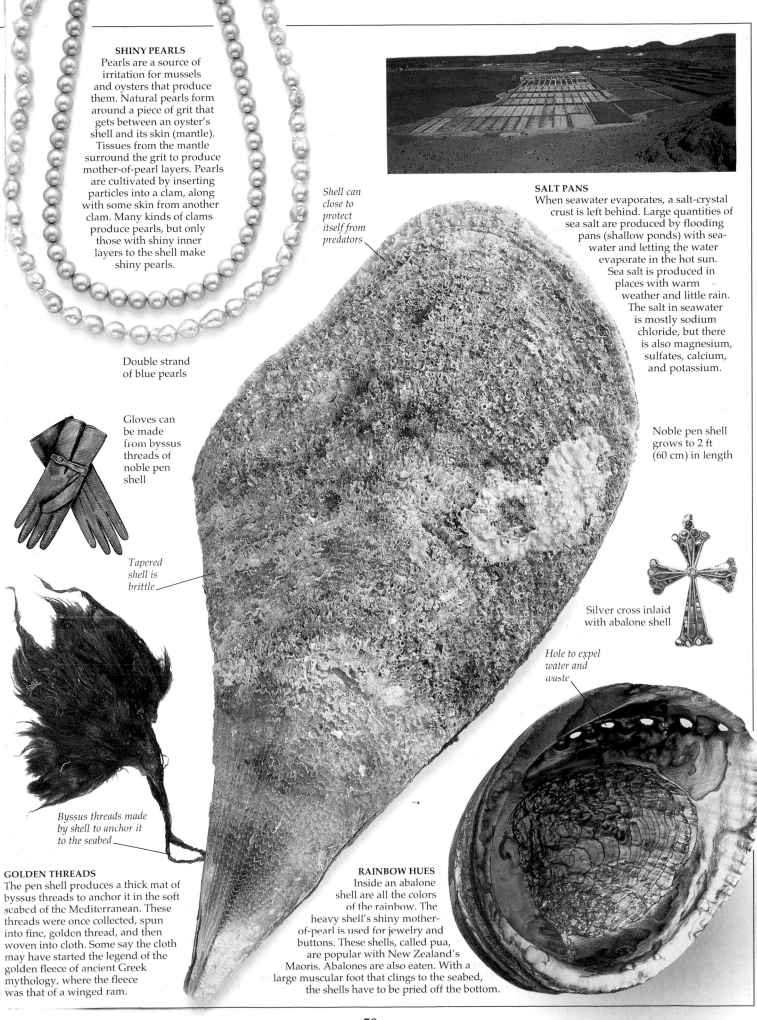

SHINY PEARLS
Pearls are a source of irritation for mussels and oysters that produce them. Natural pearls form around a piece of grit that gets between an oyster's shell and its skin (mantle). Tissues from the mantle surround the grit to produce mother-of-pearl layers. Pearls are cultivated by inserting particles into a clam, along with some skin from another clam. Many kinds of clams produce pearls, but only those with shiny inner layers to the shell make shiny pearls.

Double strand of blue pearls

Shell can close to protect itself from predators

Gloves can be made from byssus threads of noble pen shell

Tapered shell is brittle

Byssus threads made by shell to anchor it to the seabed

GOLDEN THREADS
The pen shell produces a thick mat of byssus threads to anchor it in the soft seabed of the Mediterranean. These threads were once collected, spun into fine, golden thread, and then woven into cloth. Some say the cloth may have started the legend of the golden fleece of ancient Greek mythology, where the fleece was that of a winged ram.

SALT PANS
When seawater evaporates, a salt-crystal crust is left behind. Large quantities of sea salt are produced by flooding pans (shallow ponds) with sea-water and letting the water evaporate in the hot sun. Sea salt is produced in places with warm weather and little rain. The salt in seawater is mostly sodium chloride, but there is also magnesium, sulfates, calcium, and potassium.

Noble pen shell grows to 2 ft (60 cm) in length

Silver cross inlaid with abalone shell

Hole to expel water and waste

RAINBOW HUES
Inside an abalone shell are all the colors of the rainbow. The heavy shell's shiny mother-of-pearl is used for jewelry and buttons. These shells, called pua, are popular with New Zealand's Maoris. Abalones are also eaten. With a large muscular foot that clings to the seabed, the shells have to be pried off the bottom.

Oil and gas exploration

VALUABLE RESERVOIRS OF OIL AND GAS lie hidden in rocks on the seabed. They are tapped by drilling into the rock, but first geologists must know where to drill. Only certain kinds of rocks hold oil and gas, and must be in shallow enough water to be reached by drilling. Geologists use underwater air guns and explosions on the surface to send shock waves through the seabed and distinguish between rock layers by returning signals. After a source is pinpointed, temporary rigs are set up to see if the oil is the right quality and quantity. If it is, a more permanent oil platform is built and firmly anchored to the seabed. As the oil or gas is extracted, it is off-loaded from the platform's storage tanks into larger tankers or sent ashore via pipelines. There is a great demand for oil and gas, but the earth's supplies are limited. As reservoirs dry up, new sources have to be found. Today's main offshore oil fields are in the North Sea, Gulf of Mexico, Persian Gulf, and the coasts of South America and Asia.

ON FIRE
Oil and gas are highly flammable. Despite precautions, accidents do happen, like the North Sea's Piper Alpha disaster in 1988 when 167 people died. Since then safety measures have been improved.

MILK ROUND
Helicopters deliver supplies to oil platforms far out at sea. Up to 400 people can live and work on an oil platform, but fly by helicopter for breaks onshore every few weeks.

OIL PLATFORM
One of the smaller oil platforms in the North Sea has concrete legs. Platforms are built in sections on shore. The largest section is towed out to sea and tipped upright onto the seabed, then living quarters are added. A tall derrick holds drilling equipment – several pipes tipped with strong drill bits for grinding the rocks. Special mud is sent down the pipes to cool the drill bit, wash out ground-up rock, and keep oil from gushing out. Oil platforms extract oil or gas, but rigs drill wells during exploration.

Tallest structure on this platform is flare stack, for safety reasons

Flare stack for burning off any gas that rises with the oil and cannot be used

Derrick (a steel tower) holds drilling equipment

Fireproof lifeboat gives better chance of survival

Crane hoists supplies up to platform from ship

Hand rail to protect personnel

Helicopter brings fresh food and milk to the platform

Living quarters

Helicopter pad

DEATH AND DECAY
Plant and bacteria remains from ancient seas fell to the seafloor and were covered by mud layers. Heat and pressure turned them into oil, then gas, which moved up through porous rocks, to be trapped by impermeable rocks.

Impermeable rock prevents oil from traveling farther

Oil is trapped in porous reservoir rock

Porous rock that oil can pass through

Formation of fossil fuels

AT WORK
On an oil platform, some people work on deck operating the drill, while others work inside with computers. Geologists examine rock, oil, and gas samples. Mechanics keep the machinery going. There are also cooks and cleaners to look after the crew.

ON THE BOTTOM
Divers (minus Newt suits) doing repairs underwater work longer if they return to a pressurized chamber, then back into the sea, without having to decompress after each dive.

Strong structure to withstand buffeting by wind and waves

Oxygen carried in cylinders on the back

NEWT SUIT
Thick-walled suits, like the one above, resist pressure. When underwater, the diver breathes air at normal pressure, as if inside a submersible. This means a diver can go deeper without having to undergo decompression. Newt suits (above) are used in oil exploration to depths of 1,200 ft (365 m). Joints in the arms and legs allow the diver to move.

Oceans in peril

Jewelry made of teeth of great white shark, now protected in some areas

THE OCEANS AND THE LIFE THEY SUPPORT are under threat. Sewage and industrial waste are dumped and poured from pipelines into the oceans. Carrying chemicals and metals, waste creates a dangerous buildup in the food chain. Oil spills, which smother marine life, do obvious damage. Garbage dumped at sea also kills. Turtles mistake plastic bags for jellyfish, and abandoned fishing nets entangle both seabirds and sea mammals. Over-harvesting has depleted many ocean animals, from whales to fishes. Even the souvenir trade threatens coral reefs. The situation is improving, however. New laws stop ocean pollution, regulations protect marine life, and in underwater parks people can look at ocean life without disturbing it.

Opening carved like a helmet

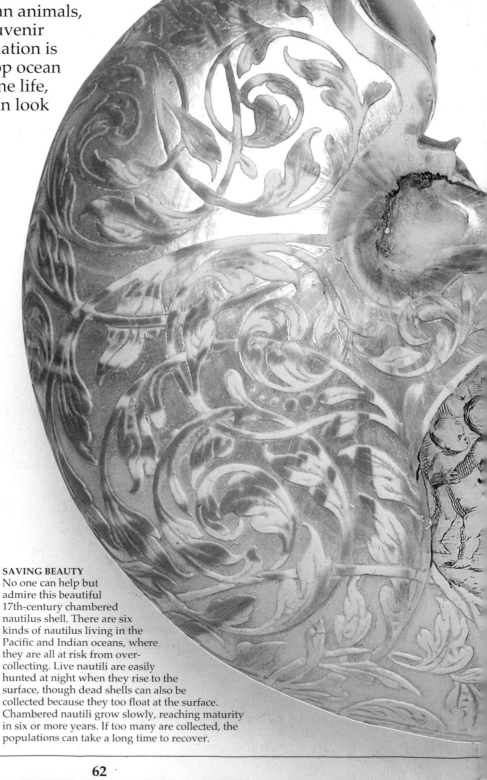

HAVE A HEART
Many people collect sea shells because of their beauty, but most shells sold in shops have been taken as living animals. If too many shelled creatures are collected from one place, such as a coral reef, the pattern of life can be disrupted. Shells should only be bought if the harvest is properly managed. It is better to go beachcombing and collect shells of already dead creatures. Always check before taking even empty shells, as some nature reserves do not permit this.

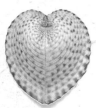

Heart cockle shells

OIL SPILL
Oil is needed for industry and motor vehicles. Huge quantities are transported at sea in tankers, sent along pipelines, and brought up from the seabed. Accidents happen and massive amounts of oil are spilled. Sea birds and sea mammals die of the cold, because their feathers or fur no longer contain pockets of air to keep them warm. Trying to clean themselves, animals die from consuming the oil, which also blocks their airways. Some are rescued, cleaned, and released back into the wild.

SAVING BEAUTY
No one can help but admire this beautiful 17th-century chambered nautilus shell. There are six kinds of nautilus living in the Pacific and Indian oceans, where they are all at risk from over-collecting. Live nautili are easily hunted at night when they rise to the surface, though dead shells can also be collected because they too float at the surface. Chambered nautili grow slowly, reaching maturity in six or more years. If too many are collected, the populations can take a long time to recover.

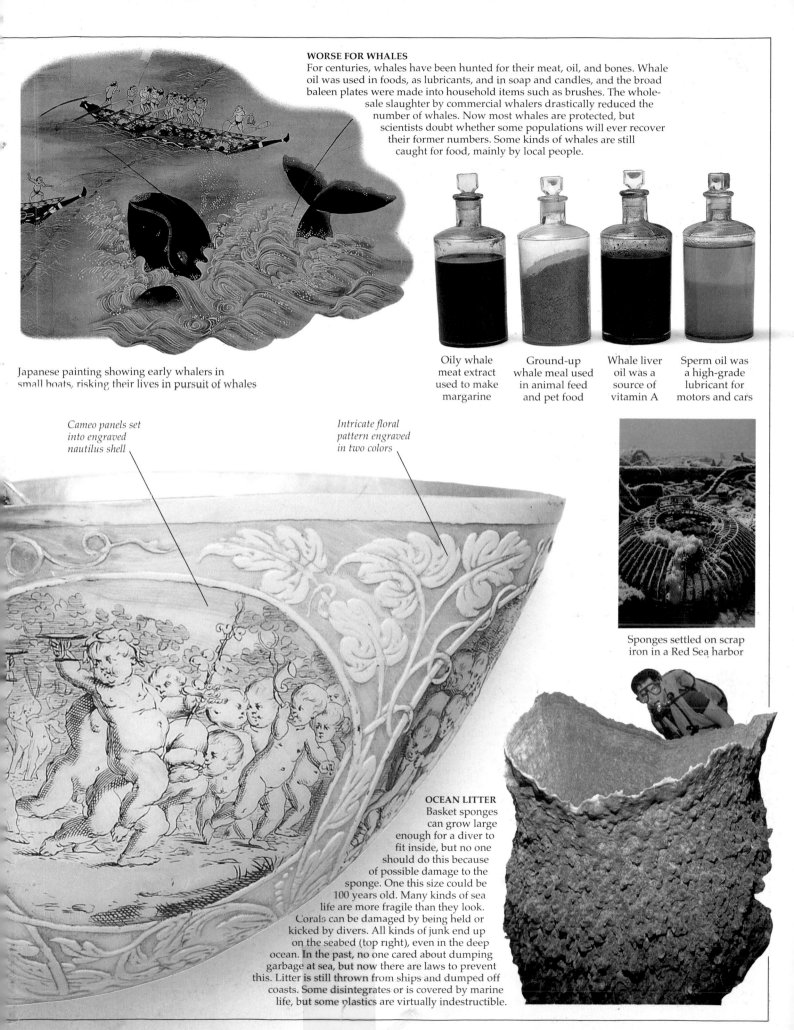

WORSE FOR WHALES

For centuries, whales have been hunted for their meat, oil, and bones. Whale oil was used in foods, as lubricants, and in soap and candles, and the broad baleen plates were made into household items such as brushes. The wholesale slaughter by commercial whalers drastically reduced the number of whales. Now most whales are protected, but scientists doubt whether some populations will ever recover their former numbers. Some kinds of whales are still caught for food, mainly by local people.

Japanese painting showing early whalers in small boats, risking their lives in pursuit of whales

Oily whale meat extract used to make margarine

Ground-up whale meal used in animal feed and pet food

Whale liver oil was a source of vitamin A

Sperm oil was a high-grade lubricant for motors and cars

Cameo panels set into engraved nautilus shell

Intricate floral pattern engraved in two colors

Sponges settled on scrap iron in a Red Sea harbor

OCEAN LITTER

Basket sponges can grow large enough for a diver to fit inside, but no one should do this because of possible damage to the sponge. One this size could be 100 years old. Many kinds of sea life are more fragile than they look. Corals can be damaged by being held or kicked by divers. All kinds of junk end up on the seabed (top right), even in the deep ocean. In the past, no one cared about dumping garbage at sea, but now there are laws to prevent this. Litter is still thrown from ships and dumped off coasts. Some disintegrates or is covered by marine life, but some plastics are virtually indestructible.

Index

Acknowledgments

Dorling Kindersley would like to thank:
For their invaluable assistance during photography: The University Marine Biological Station, Scotland, especially Prof. John Davenport, David Murden, Bobbie Wilkie, Donald Patrick, Phil Lonsdale, Ken Cameron, Dr. Jason Hall-Spencer, Simon Thurston, Steve Parker, Geordie Campbell, and Helen Thirlwall. Sea Life Centres (UK), especially Robin James, David Copp, Patrick van der Merwe, and Ian Shaw (Weymouth); and Marcus Goodsir (Portsmouth). Colin Pelton, Peter Hunter, Dr. Brian Bett, and Mike Conquer of the Institute of Oceanographic Sciences. Tim Parmenter, Simon Caslaw, and Paul Ruddock of the Natural History Museum, London. Margaret Bidmead of the Royal Navy Submarine Museum, Gosport. IFREMER for their kind permission to photograph the model of *Nautile*.

David Fowler of Deep Sea Adventure. Mark Graham, Andrew and Richard Pierson of Otterferry Salmon Ltd. Bob Donaldson of Angus Modelmakers. Sally Rose for additional research. Kathy Lockley for providing props. Helena Spiteri, Djinn von Noorden, Susan St. Louis, Ivan Finnegan, Joe Hoyle, Mark Haygarth, and David Pickering for editorial and design assistance.

Special photography: Ray Möller; Steve Gorton

Model makers: Peter Griffiths and David Donkin

Artwork: John Woodcock and Simone End

Index: Hilary Bird

Picture credits
(l=left r=right t=top b=below c=center a=above)
American Museum of Natural History 11tl (no. 419(2)).
Heather Angel 38bc.
Ardea/Val Taylor 62tl.
Tracey Bowden/Pedro Borrell 55tc.
Bridgeman Art Library/Prado, Madrid 9tr; Uffizi Gallery, Florence: 16tr.
British Museum 54tr.
Cable & Wireless Archive 44tr.
Bruce Coleman Ltd/Carl Roessler 22c; Frieder Sauer 26tr; Charles & Sandra Hood 27tc; Jeff Foott 28tr, 56tr; Jane Burton 38bl; Michael Roggo 57 tl; Orion Service & Trading Co. 58br; Atlantide SDF 59tr; Nancy Sefton 63br.
Steven J. Cooling 61tr.
Mary Evans Picture Library 11tr, 12tr, 19tl, 20tl, 28tl, 33tr, 34tr, 40cl, 45tr, 48tr, 49tl, 50bl, 52tr, 54c, 60tl.
Ronald Grant Archive 42cl, 55bl.
Robert Harding Picture Library 25tl, 32tr, 32bc, 39br, 57tr, 63tl.
Institute of Oceanographic Sciences 46lc.
© Japanese Meteorological Agency/Meteorological Office 12l.
Frank Lane Photo Agency/M. Newman 11br.
Simon Conway Morris 6tr.
N.H.P.A./Agence Natur 44c.
Oxford Scientific Films/Toi de Roy 29tr; Fred Bavendam 43tl.
Planet Earth Pictures/Peter Scoones 9tl; Norbert Wu 10–11c, 20cl, 40tr, 40tl, 41tl, 42tr; Gary Bell 23br, 55tr; Mark Conlin 25c, 36br; Menuhin 29tc; Ken Lucas 30tl; Neville Coleman 33cr; Steve Bloom 37c; Andrew Mounter 38br; Larry Madin 43br; Ken Vaughan 51cr; Georgette Doowma 63cr.
Science Photo Library/Dr. G. Feldman 26bl; Ron Church 53cr; Simon Fraser 62bl.
Frank Spooner Pictures 47tr, 47cr, 54br, 54bl, 60tr, 60cr.
Tony Stone Images, Jeff Rotman 53lc.
Stolt Comex Seaway Ltd 61l.
Town Docks Museum, Hull 63tr.
ZEFA 36cl, 56ct.
Every effort has been made to trace the copyright holders of photographs. The publishers apologize for any omissions and will amend further editions.